HIS HOLINESS

MAHARISHI
MAHESH YOGI

A Living Saint
for the New Millennium

Stories of his first visit to the USA

Told by Helena and Roland Olson

Special Commemorative Edition

Los Angeles, California 1967
2nd Edition Los Angeles, California 1979
3rd Edition Fairfield, Iowa 2000

Published by
1st World Library
1100 N 4TH STREET
Fairfield, IA 52556
1-641-209-5000
www.1stworldpublishing.com

ISBN 1-59540-993-9
LCCN: 2004091009

®Transcendental Meditation, TM, TM-Sidhi, Maharishi TM,
Maharishi Transcendental Meditation,
Maharishi TM-Sidhi, and Word of Wisdom are registered
or common law trademarks licensed to
Maharishi Vedic Education Development Corporation
and used with permission.

Written for
THOSE WHO LOVE HIM

Dedicated to Maharishi,

whose humility, gentleness, wisdom, nobility

and sustaining love led the way

to the path of Enlightenment.

I wish to express my love and deep appreciation to the

Los Angeles members of the Spiritual Regeneration Movement,

who were first in the Western Hemisphere

to support Maharishi Mahesh Yogi in teaching

his simple technique of Transcendental Meditation®.

Contents

Appendices

Preface to the Third Edition **by Theresa Olson**

———————◆●◆———————

Forty years ago, in May of 1959, His Holiness Maharishi Mahesh Yogi first visited the United States of America. It seems only fitting to bring out a commemorative edition of the book written by my mother in 1967 wherein she described the adventures of Maharishi's first summer in this country. It is a book so like Maharishi, a tender story told simply about a great man with a superhuman goal.

During these forty years, I have had the opportunity to quietly witness this great man going about the manifestation of a phenomenal vision—a vision based on the principle that everyone should naturally and innocently live 200 percent of life: one hundred percent inner spiritual joy along with one hundred percent outer material satisfaction. Maharishi wanted to bring humankind out of suffering and restore to us our rightful human dignity. He envisioned a world in which its citizens could enjoy a life free from problems—an ideal life based in good, useful and virtuous thoughts, words and actions; where we could enjoy the blessings of spontaneous good health, excellent and effective systems of education for our children, increased economic prosperity, and improved

I

social well-being on all levels of society; where the spiritual ideals of all religions could be realized and lived in daily life; and, most importantly, where we could live in lasting world peace and real friendship with one another. And Maharishi offered a simple, powerful solution for realizing that goal—an easy, natural, mental technique that he called Transcendental Meditation, which allows anyone to develop his or her full potential while simultaneously nourishing the surrounding environment.

Maharishi has tirelessly traveled the globe, offering the same sweet message that he spoke to my parents and their generation in our living room so many years ago, to anyone who would listen. For the millions who did listen, they automatically began to live the fruits of the promise which Maharishi made in 1959.

Maharishi has remained true to his promise. For those individuals who regularly practice his Transcendental Meditation technique and also his advanced programs, these characteristics of inner and outer growth in daily life have become obvious. TM® works, not only for the middle class, but also for the upper classes of society as well as for the poor and underprivileged. TM works, regardless of the color of our skin, the language that we speak, the country that we live in, the religion that we practice. TM works, whether we are man or woman, child, teenager, working adult or retired. TM works for all humans, whether we are free or incarcerated, literate or illiterate, employed or unemployed. The main point is: TM really does work, just like Maharishi said it would.

But don't take just his word for it. During these past forty years, Maharishi has asked scientists from such prestigious universities as Harvard, Yale, Stanford, UC Berkeley, UCLA and others around the world, to rigorously test the benefits of his Transcendental Meditation technique. Now, there are more than 600 scientific studies, available in six volumes of *Scientific Research on Maharishi's Transcendental Meditation and TM-Sidhi Program, Collected Papers*, documenting the benefits of this technique for every area of society. In her book, Mother mentioned some of the practical benefits that Maharishi originally predicted in 1959. I have updated the documented evidence in this edition that demonstrates the validity of Maharishi's earliest predictions scientifically. Explanatory notes and charts illustrating this scientific evidence appear in the Appendices.

Maharishi has also spent a lot of time addressing the theoretical underpinnings of an ideal society and the characteristics of an ideal administration that would govern such a society. Again, scientific evidence corroborates his early predictions from 1959, indicating that the Transcendental Meditation technique is a viable means for creating world peace, for decreasing violence in society, for augmenting all good in our society and for allowing us to manage our stress in such a way as to beneficially help others while simultaneously helping ourselves.

Maharishi has talked about the strengths and weaknesses of educational systems from around the world. During his global travels yearly for over twenty-five years, Maharishi observed first-hand what worked and what didn't. He researched a system of education used when an ideal society existed on earth thousands of years ago—the time of a Vedic civilization—and found many more strengths than weaknesses in that system when compared to modern systems. Because of those strengths, Maharishi reformulated the principles of Vedic education for modern society and has made a system of Consciousness-Based℠ education available in his schools and universities around the world.

Talk to students at these universities and schools. Ask them their impressions of this Vedic system of education. Surprisingly, students like it. Not only do students learn objective information, but also, through their regular practice of the Transcendental Meditation technique, students experience the source of all knowledge within their own awareness. Because of this experience students find that they can grasp and relate personally to profound abstract concepts. The Vedic principle of self-referral helps to explain why.

According to Maharishi this beautiful principle of self-referral says that knowledge is not outside of me, but rather inside of me. In its purest expression it resides at the source of all thought, the field of pure consciousness, the Unified Field of Natural Law; and That, in its essential nature, actually constitutes my mental and physical structure. I am pure knowledge; my self-consciousness is essentially the Self as Consciousness, the I-ness, Am-ness and Is-ness taught in Western philosophy, in world religions, and ultimately in the most abstract forms of physical and biological sciences. In the West, experience of this state is considered unattainable by most of us. Maharishi teaches that not only is experience of this state attainable in a systematic way for all of us through regular practice of his Transcendental Meditation technique, but also knowledge and experience of it can be incorporated into a system of Consciousness-Based education to ensure that students grow up with the experience of self-referral fully established in their individual awareness.

This natural, systematic experience of self-referral consciousness makes all knowledge meaningful, relevant and important, in a way that other systems of education can never accomplish. Maharishi saw the possibility of this kind of education back in 1959; again, I have included information that shows its practical applications to society as numbered references in the original text.

Maharishi has been on the cutting edge of this rediscovery of good in the ancient Vedic knowledge and approaches to life. He has made the best of that knowledge available in a modern format suitable to life in this modern age. His Vedic system of education is one example of knowledge based on this principle. Others include his Vedic approach to health, to agriculture, and to construction of homes and office buildings.

As Maharishi's TM Movement expanded around the world, a need arose for larger and more suitable accommodations. From our simple home, Maharishi moved into larger hotels in Europe where he could train teachers of the Transcendental Meditation technique. At times these courses numbered over three thousand participants. Older hotels were bought and renovated and then generous individuals invited Maharishi to stay there to oversee the administration of his global Movement. Even these have proved too small. The needs of the Movement have grown so greatly that now the construction of the world's tallest building is underway to care for Maharishi and his global administrative staff.

Perhaps the most precious contribution in the book is my mother's own discovery of the compatibility of the theoretical knowledge and practical experience of the Transcendental Meditation program with the practice of one's own religion. Our family faith was Roman Catholic. My mother also had a degree in philosophy from UCLA. With her inquiring mind, she probed deeply, and checked and confirmed for herself that TM actually supported all aspects of religious life. For my mother, her practice of the Transcendental Meditation technique supplemented and enriched her religious faith. In addition, she found that Maharishi showed a profound understanding of the fundamental beliefs of the Christian faith. In fact, Maharishi's great respect for the founders of all religions is an example for us all. He naturally appreciates the universal values found in each religion. Although he remains true to his own faith, at no time does he impose his faith on others. He simply appreciates the great good found in each.

For those who need, I have included some personal statements from various individuals who represent the world religions and who also practice the Maharishi Transcendental Meditation^{SM} technique regularly. They know better than I do what it means to practice both; whether or not there is a conflict; or, if practice of the Transcendental Meditation technique actually complements the practice of religion. Please read what they have to say if you have any questions. For me, personally, the Transcendental Meditation program has given me the key to open the door to the kingdom of heaven within. God and belief in God and worship of God is very important in my life. The Transcendental Meditation program and its advanced Vedic technologies have helped me develop spiritually so that I can better appreciate what it means to worship God and to better understand the magnificence of God's creation. And that has given me a clearer understanding of my own responsibility in using God's creation, our earth and its natural resources, wisely.

Acknowledgments

There are many people that I would like to thank for helping with this commemorative edition. First, I would like to thank my sister, Christina Sterling, and her beloved husband, Peter, for agreeing to print a third edition. Their constant support actually inspired me to consider undertaking and completing this project. I would also like to thank Dr. Kumuda Reddy for her willingness to print this book through her Samhita Productions Company. Her understanding for the need of this book and her financial backing have made this book possible. She is a wonderful human being and friend and I will be eternally grateful to her.

I would also like to thank those who personally worked on the book: Stuart Friedman for his brilliant cover design; Tony Ellis for his superb organizing power and gentle prodding to get something to him; Tracy Liptak for her careful editing—if you read and understand, Tracy made that possible.

I would like to thank the contributors: Fr. Kevin Joyce, Rabbi Allen Green, Rev. John Reigstad, Mr. Wadi Buonnaur, Mrs. Sooneeta Chatturagoon Eisen, and Mr. Paul Frank for their personal experiences regarding TM and religion.

I would also to thank my husband, John W. Sorflaten, Ph.D., C.P.E., whose constant love and compassion inspired me to stay on task. Without John there would be no book.

I would like to thank the administrators of Maharishi University of Management who assisted in getting necessary approvals for updated information on the Transcendental Meditation program used in the book: Dr. Bevan Morris, President, for his sincerity and trust in my ability to do a good job; Martha Bright for getting me copies of scientific charts to use in the book; and most importantly, the Psychology Department at Maharishi University of Management, of which I am a faculty member, for their continued enthusiastic support in my producing the book. I would like to especially thank Dr. Fred Travis, Chairman of the Psychology Department, and his wonderful wife, Nita, for constantly being there and believing in me to do this project. No matter what I needed, Fred said yes and then figured out how to make that happen. And, interestingly, it was Nita who really inspired me to actually get to work when she told me that she liked to have her children read the book before going to sleep. Since Avery Travis is my godchild, I felt a special responsibility to put in her hands a really good book about someone whom she loves very much—Maharishi. Thank you Nita and Fred for being such wonderful friends.

Lastly, I would like to thank the hero of this book, His Holiness Maharishi Mahesh Yogi. Maharishi, at all times and in all places, has been my guiding light and inspiration. He exemplifies in his own life the goals of his public message.

To meet Maharishi, to know him as I have for the last forty years, is to have the blessings of a gift incomparable to all others. His love transcends continental boundaries; his effulgence surpasses the brilliance of diamonds; his genius eclipses Einstein's; his holiness in thought and action sets the highest standard of spirituality for the world. He lives 200 percent of life with no difficulty whatsoever. Coupled with all that is an immeasurable charm and graciousness, a boundless compassion for suffering humanity and a superb sense of good humor. Maharishi, one person, has united people the world over in a global purpose: to improve the quality of life on every level of society by first improving the quality of life of each individual in society.

And to think that I grew up in his shadow—a child quietly observing and learning and appreciating all that this great man has to offer. He's a marvelous role model for young people. I lived at his feet, learning about life from this living saint from the Himalayas, who left his own quiet lifestyle to live in the noisy, flashy society of the last half of the twentieth century. His transition from utter silence to incredible activity was so natural, completely harmonious and balanced. His actions and behaviors betray his noble state of enlightenment.

In those beginning years, we had no idea what Maharishi had to offer, but we liked him and his message. And we decided that we wanted to experience for ourselves that which he described. This desire was all we needed to start on the path towards gaining our own enlightenment. Maharishi's goal is our enlightenment. His nourishing yet unobtrusive care to help us attain that goal has continued ceaselessly over the years. His care is unselfish, and very real. We just need to recognize it for what it is.

Maharishi, thank you. You have shared your vision and have taught so many of us how to attain the highest human goal possible. You have established a Movement to preserve the purity of your teaching for time immemorial. You have poured your heart and soul into the creation of this phenomenal Vedic system of education, ensuring that the children of succeeding generations will never need to suffer. And you did that because you cared for our well-being.

How can a blossoming flower thank the gardener for his compassionate, ever-nourishing care? Only by blooming fully and thereby bringing satisfaction to the gardener's heart.

The *Bhagavad-Gita* is a Vedic textbook of knowledge in which Lord Krishna enlightens the great warrior, Arjuna, in the matter of a few hours through a profound dialogue—a form of Vedic Counseling. In Chapter Three, Lord Krishna describes the effects that a great man has on others when He says:

> *Whatsoever a great man does, the very*
> *same is also done by other men.*
> *Whatever standard he sets,*
> *the world follows it.*
> *Bhagavad-Gita 3.21*

Maharishi has set the highest standards and we are following—following a living Saint into the glorious new millennium.

Theresa M. Olson, Ph.D.
August 15, 1999
On the occasion of my 40th anniversary
of learning the Transcendental
Meditation technique.

NOTE: Throughout the book, you will find Transcendental Meditation referred to as the Transcendental Meditation technique, TM, or Maharishi Transcendental Meditation. All refer to the same technique. See Appendix A for a brief definition of the technique.

Preface to the Second Edition **by Theresa Olson**

———————— ◆ ● ◆ ————————

August 15, 1959, I walked into the study to wish Maharishi good morning. Ten minutes later, I walked out with a treasure: my very own secret "Word of Wisdom^{SM}."

At age ten that was the beginning of my life in the TM Movement made possible by the open-heartedness and love of my dear parents.

Back then, however, my thoughts revolved more around the tempting fruit brought by the new meditators that lay lusciously in baskets all through the house than it did with the TM Movement. I would play all day and then go to lectures given by an Indian Yogi at night—not totally understanding what he said about refining our awareness and living 200 percent of life—100 percent spiritual and 100 percent material—but enjoying every minute of his talks all the same. Now, twenty years later, I am totally committed to Maharishi's global endeavor to raise world consciousness to enlightenment.

I literally grew up with this international movement. At about the time when we were studying foreign lands in geography at school, Maharishi was bringing the citizens of these lands to '433,' our address on Harvard Boulevard in Los Angeles at that time. Long before others my age were concerned with the social problems of the world, I was listening to deep thoughts on consciousness and on how to raise it through TM, and what we could then expect to see happen socially. Consequently, all the social good—the move away from potential world-wide disaster toward global enlightenment—that has developed in the last few years, I naturally consider to be the result of more people practicing Maharishi Transcendental Meditation^SM. After all, Maharishi did say that this would happen way back then, and it has.

My first impressions of Maharishi: someone kind and real and wholly there, someone who did not hide behind the pretext of being an adult. Someone who knew the real me—not the "me" who acted and talked and played roles. Maharishi was very real to me, then, in a way that only children can understand. That reality has never changed.

Maybe his looks have changed, and his focus has shifted from the individual to the society, but his essential nature—his essential reality—is still the same now as it was then.

Somehow, my mother has captured his essence in this book.

It was Mother's desire, before she passed away in 1975, to update and republish her book in the United States. Now we are able to fulfill that desire.

For this second edition, however, we have made a few changes and additions.

As Maharishi's TM Movement grew and expanded, the expressions used to illustrate certain points changed; we have changed these expressions accordingly.

The title has been changed to honor, acknowledge and better identify who it is about and when.

We have added appendices that validate Maharishi's predictions about the TM technique which he made in 1959.

In order to preserve the charm of the original story, we have put all footnote references in the back. These footnotes, we feel, prove Maharishi's prognostications coming true. It is incredible how many ambitious plans were made in 1959, and how easily they have been realized since then.

We would like to thank several people for their help in getting this second edition printed: Carol Young for her typing skills, the Executive Governors of the Age of Enlightenment in California for their uplifting encouragement and support of this project, Ellen Wohl and Pat Hirsch for their editorial suggestions, and Peter Warburton for so gently untangling the red tape.

Our gratitude also goes to Maharishi for giving my sister, Christina, and me the wisdom to see the value of our mother's book in the Age of Enlightenment, and for his blessings in re-printing it at this time.

In order to bring the story completely up to date, mention must be made of the TM-Sidhi® program which Maharishi made available to the world in 1977. It is the latest step in Maharishi's program to bring enlightenment to the world.

The TM-Sidhi program fully activates our human potential as seen in the ability to perform such supernormal feats as flying, developing enhanced hearing, and being able to perceive one's own, inner bodily system. Scientific research attributes the successful performance of these feats to the development of perfect mind-body coordination (scientists carrying out research in this field have called it the optimizing of brain functioning) brought about by regular practice of the Maharishi TM^{SM} and TM-Sidhi programs.

What is the difference between Transcendental Meditation and the TM-Sidhi program? We know that with regular practice of Transcendental Meditation, we become familiar with the state of pure, unbounded awareness, the field of all possibilities, the ground state of natural law. This is a field of pure potential. With the Maharishi TM-Sidhi program, we start to actualize that potential, because we learn how to function from the level of pure, unbounded awareness. The result is spontaneous fulfillment of desires. If the mind says to fly, the body responds. Any desire that is in accord with natural law is spontaneously fulfilled, if one can think it from the state of pure, unbounded awareness. As a matter of fact, greater fulfillment of desires is a common experience for those who practice the Maharishi TM and TM-Sidhi programs.

To date, over 4,000 people, men and women, from all walks of life and from all lands, have learned the TM-Sidhi technique. These "Governors and Citizens of the Age of Enlightenment" are known for their friendliness, their mental coherence, their good health and success in business and education.

Why did Maharishi introduce the TM-Sidhi program at this time?

The effects of his Transcendental Meditation program on world consciousness have already been felt by 140 countries in terms of their improved quality of life. The trends of time have changed from riots, sit-ins, assassinations, and the threat of World War III to the sunshine of the Age of Enlightenment. In the last 20 years, people everywhere have become aware of their inner selves and of the need for developing their full potential. Today, we are taking care of our health naturally, eating better foods, learning to balance rest and activity. We are expanding the boundaries of our awareness and are culturing and strengthening our minds. We are learning how to integrate our inner life with our outer. We are waking up to the joy of living 200 percent of life totally in accord with natural law.

Why, then, the TM-Sidhi program?

Maharishi brought out the TM-Sidhi program because we deserved it. Up until this time, these sidhis would have been seen as just so much magic, as illusions. By the late 1970s, however, the quality of world consciousness had improved just enough so that we could appreciate the TM-Sidhi program for what it is: a milestone of achievement in the development of higher states of consciousness. Consequently, Maharishi was able to give us this great gift which accelerates enlightenment in the individual.

With our expanded awareness, we are now capable of performing the TM-Sidhi program naturally, without any strain. And as world consciousness continues to rise in coherence, we will be able to even more fully comprehend and appreciate the great value of this program in stabilizing higher states of consciousness.

A few individuals, about one percent of the adult population, practicing the Maharishi TM and TM-Sidhi programs, generate a tremendous influence on the whole of society. As they enliven the ground state of natural law, they automatically increase harmony, coherence, and orderliness in their own awareness. At the same time, these evolutionary impulses radiate throughout the entire society, producing collective coherence, dissolving collective stress, and thereby neutralizing the basis of all conflict and violence. The result is a sudden, effortless transformation in the nation—from violent uprisings and revolutions to harmony and peace. Herein lies the greatest contribution of the TM-Sidhi program to mankind—an invincible method for achieving world peace!

Does it work?

In October, 1978, the World Government of the Age of Enlightenment, under Maharishi's guidance, sent Governors of the Age of Enlightenment to restore peace in the five most troubled areas of the world. Six weeks later, the violence and negativity in these areas had completely calmed down. According to reports, when the Governors of the Age of Enlightenment started withdrawing from these areas, violence once more threatened to flare up. The World Government responded by sending more Governors to the area to preserve an orderly, peaceful environment, and violence again calmed down. Coherence produced in these individuals did, indeed, affect the society.

Now people around the world are learning the Maharishi TM and TM-Sidhi programs so that the citizens of every country will be able to prevent any future crises or eruptions of violence from arising, thereby contributing to the establishment of permanent world peace.

Maharishi has structured the TM-Sidhi course for TM program meditators which are easy to take, enjoyable, interesting, and adaptable to busy schedules. Meditators can find out more about these "Citizen Advanced Courses" at their local TM Program Centers.

What has Transcendental Meditation done for me?

Transcending thought and diving into unbounded, pure awareness for so many years has structured an inner silence deep within that proves to be unshakable even in the roughest circumstances. It is as if an anchor is attached to a boat in a stormy sea, keeping the boat safe, secure and stable. Having this inner silence allows me to act in a more coherent way throughout the entire day. As a result I am more flexible, capable of adapting to the changing times, while inside I remain stable and calm. My health has improved; my mind is clearer and sharper; I am more appreciative of others.

I, like many others, have experienced that during the practice of the TM and TM-Sidhi programs consciousness fluctuates as superfluid waves extending beyond the finite boundaries of body, home, surroundings, world and even this galaxy until they finally merge with the unbounded, unmanifest impulses of creative intelligence which are found to be the root of all creation.

This expansion of consciousness beyond boundaries brings an exulting sense of freedom, of fulfillment; and along with that comes the feeling that I can be and do anything that I desire.

But this invincible feeling of the mind is tempered by a simultaneous expansion of the heart—a gentle cushioning of infinite love for the entire creation that locates one's self as the Self within everything.

These experiences, so common to those who practice Maharishi Transcendental Meditation, are just the beginning of the explorations into inner space. So much more is there; and with the blessings of Maharishi, and the wisdom of the ancient Veda coupled with the findings of modern science, it will soon be ours.

The story that my mother has recorded here is true. I remember so clearly asking her, "What in the world is a Yogi?" on that early May morning so long ago as she wrote it on page 38. As a child Mother had a photographic mind. In later years, whenever she wanted, she could totally recall any situation accurately. It is interesting for those of us who were there to remember certain instances and then check them against Mother's story and find them true.

In a way, this is her gift to all of you: the gift of sharing and of making you a part of those intimate, early days when Maharishi was at '433'.

Jai Guru Dev
Theresa M. Olson
Los Angeles, California
March, 1978

Introduction

Sometimes a house sits on a street for years and years and years and not much happens to it. It changes ownership every decade or so, because the children in a family grow up and seek new places. If it is allowed to sit there patiently a new cycle starts for it, and then the graciousness of age combines with the vitality of youth. The family who lives in such a place is fortunate indeed.

From 1950 to 1952 my husband Roland and myself had been searching for the right home. His special assignment with the Telephone Company, which had necessitated our living in the suburbs, was finished. Now he was back at the downtown office in Los Angeles, and we were glad to get back to the conveniences of city life. We had not rushed as our eldest daughter, Melinda, was in her last years of high school. With her graduation in 1952 house-hunting became serious.

When we saw the two-story, Cape Cod, gray-shingled house on Harvard Boulevard, it was love at first sight. We saw the house one day; the next day we started moving in, and soon the younger children were playing hide-and-go-seek behind the big, old trees. My husband, myself, our four girls (ages eighteen to four), their pets and friends accepted '433', as it was nicknamed, as a member of the family. And, in time, '433' became known and loved in many cities and far-off places.

"When we saw the two-story Cape Cod gray-shingled house, it was love at first sight."

Roland, the house and myself shared a secret. We all started life in the same year, 1909. By 1959, with the marriages of the two oldest girls, we were beginning to think of less activity. Now and then we mentioned retirement, thinking our active days would soon be over. We couldn't have been more mistaken; but then, how could we know that a Yogi was leaving the Himalayas in India, and after some travelling, would join our family circle at '433'? Never did a more puzzled East meet a more uninformed West than Maharishi and those who were drawn to him.

The amusing and sometimes embarrassing every-day incidents, a glimpse of a charming personality, and a desire to share his words of wisdom are the reason for this book.

Chapter One It Happened in Hollywood

Our children were different from other people's children in one way: other people's children brought home stray dogs and cats— ours brought home people!

Of course, like everything else, somewhere along the line the parents set the example, and I must plead guilty in this instance. In 1952, from the first day our family of four daughters moved into '433' (as we lovingly called the old 16-room home on Harvard Boulevard) we had extra people in the house. The first was a widower friend of ours who couldn't find the right person to look after his twelve-year-old daughter. We took them in until he could find a housekeeper, never dreaming he would soon marry a widow with one child and a dog who would all come to "stay a while." As soon as they were gone to a nice home of their own, a long procession of young actors, dancers, students, teachers, singers and even the Ballet Master of Sadler's Wells (a famous British ballet company) made their home with us for a few days, weeks, months and in one case, a year.

Our eldest daughter, Melinda, was responsible for the theatrical group as she, before her marriage, had a promising career in the theater. It didn't get beyond "promising" but it was interesting. Mary, our second daughter, and a graduate of the University of California at Los Angeles, was responsible for the students. My husband Roland was responsible...for the bills!

By 1959, Tina, age 15, had taken over the top spot in the house and carried on a vigorous protest against more company. She said, "It's too much work to have company. Nobody helps with the dishes, especially Theresa!"

With this direct thrust at ten-year-old Theresa she generally vanished into her part of the house with her two Siamese cats, Mei-Ling and Su-Ling.

Theresa, a friendly but quiet little girl who enjoyed everything in life—babies, animals, old and young people, entertainment and food—always managed somehow to escape the dishes.

Even though our company had been a little bother, each in his own way enriched our lives. We received a firsthand report on two or three sects of Protestantism (we were Catholic), Christian Science, New Thought, Spiritualism, Hypnotism, and all the arts. Conversations in our old-fashioned kitchen were lively and often heated. Discussion never lagged as the dishes mounted up!

In April of 1959, much to Tina's delight, we were temporarily "out of company." But, accustomed to constant discussion and discourses, Roland and I had been stimulated to attend many lectures on a great variety of subjects, and we were reading books on subjects we never knew existed.

It was through the reading of one of these books that we came to have the most delightful experience of our lives...the meeting with a Master—Maharishi Mahesh Yogi.

The book had something to do with Masters from the Far East. After quickly glancing through it I remarked to my husband:

"The book was written by an engineer who went to India. He met yogis and sages who do miraculous things like walking on water. Doesn't that sound interesting?"

"Doesn't sound like engineering to me," said my husband, who had a degree in science. "All that could be fakery."

For that reason we decided not to buy the book.

However, my husband surprised me with the very same book within a few days.

"Someone handed it to me in the office. Thought we might enjoy it," he said.

It was a small book and easy to read.

Part of it must be fiction, I thought to myself; but I rather think there is a lot of fact here. Anyway, it is fascinating, and I would like to know more about Masters and the East.

I reviewed it briefly for the family at dinner. The next day I bought more books on the subject. I reported to the family at the dinner table.

"You might be interested to know there are people in the Orient who live on light alone. It seems they rise at three or four in the morning in parts of the Himalayas and breathe a certain way. They are sustained entirely until the next day."

"Think of the dishes that would save," said Tina.

"Even better than that, if anyone is hungry, they merely reach into the air and bring out a hot meal."

I couldn't blame the family for being a bit skeptical. Besides, something was lost in the telling of it.

"You should all read the books," I said.

I finished the set on the last Friday of April. On Saturday, on the back page of the women's section of the *Times,* there was a small ad which read:

Maharishi Mahesh Yogi
From the Himalayas
Will speak at the Masquers Club
May 1 to May 5 Phone....

"Imagine that," I said to my husband, "and the fascinating thing about it is that a Master from the East is at the Hollywood Actors Club! Quite a contrast! Would you like to go and hear him?"

Roland thought for a moment. "It sounds interesting. Let's give it a try."

His Holiness
MAHARISHI MAHESH YOGI
FROM THE HIMALAYAS
One of India's foremost spiritual leaders, on world tour, now comes to Los Angeles to reveal his HIMALAYAN DISCOVERY of a simple technique by which everyone can easily utilize the tremendous forces of the inner self to secure ABUNDANCE, MENTAL TRANQUILITY, MORE VITAL ENERGY AND REAL HAPPINESS in the fast tempo of modern living.
HIS HOLINESS WILL SPEAK at 8:00 until 9:30 P.M., May 1, 2, 3, 4 and 5 and at 10:30 A.M. until noon, May 2 and 3 at the MASQUERS CLUB, 1765 No. Sycamore Ave., HOLLYWOOD. Seats reserved by request.
For Information and Private Interviews Phone HO. 5-2985

The original advertisement displayed in the Los Angeles Times that caught my mother's attention and led her to attend Maharishi's first lecture in Los Angeles.

So I phoned the number in the ad. A pleasant male voice answered. I told him that we would be coming. He seemed surprised and a bit relieved. As there are no large lecture rooms in the Masquers Club, I asked if it would be necessary to come early.

"I don't think so," he said. "So far, you're the only one who has called."

I felt unhappy. Having worked in a theater for the past six years, I was overwhelmed with a desire to "get out and sell tickets." In our circle of friends I couldn't think of anyone I could ask to go along. I fretted about it all day Sunday. Finally, my husband said, "Stop worrying about it. It's not your problem. It's a good sign they'll have a packed house."

"Of course. You're right. It's only when you think you have an audience that no one comes to the theater."

We ate early Monday evening, said nothing to the family about where we were going and set out. It was the first time in my life I arrived early for a lecture. The thought of a Master from the Far East at the Hollywood Actors Club was exhilarating. I could hardly wait.

We always enjoyed studying the crowds at lectures, as no doubt they did us. My husband and I generally looked a bit "ordinary" wherever we went. But tonight the entire group of about 40 or 45 persons seemed to be just plain business people. Some were young, but most were close to our age, moderate in taste and dress.

We were assembled in the lounge. Comfortable armchairs were arranged in a semi-circle facing a small stage. A little bench with a deerskin draped over it was directly under dozens of pictures of Hollywood's greatest male stars. In front of the bench were two or three vases full of flowers. A modern tape recorder and speaker were close to the bench.

"None of it seems real," I whispered to my husband.

There was not much conversation. A nice looking young man came out and checked the tape recorder. Then, from a side door, the Master entered.

Walking toward us slowly, with calm dignity, was a man slight in build and short in stature, clothed in white silk seamless robes, a brown shawl around his shoulders.

It seemed as though someone breathed, "Oh!" But there was no desire to speak or think, only to look again and again to try to see something we could not define.

In his hands he held beautiful roses. A serene face looked out from under long, silky black hair that fell around his shoulders. A full growth of beard covered his chin. We were utterly fascinated as he slipped delicate brown feet from wooden sandals and sat crosslegged on the deerskin.

He sat silently fingering some beads worn around his neck. We were quiet and comfortable. I had an intense desire to look into his eyes, but for a long time he did not look up.

Poor man. Such a long way from home. Such a distance for minds to bridge. What will he talk about? I thought.

He cleared his throat a little and opened his eyes. Large, luminous, brown eyes travelled to each person in the room, almost in greeting. I wanted so much to have him look at me, and he did...the last one. I started to smile, but he began to speak at that moment.

His voice drew one's entire attention. At first it was almost

"A serene face looked out from under long, silky black hair."

without sound. The quietness of his speech seemed to direct ideas to the mind and not the ear.

He spoke of a mission which brought him out of the Valley of the Saints in India, a mission which was to say to all the world who would listen, that life is bliss, that the path to enlightenment is a blissful path, without suffering, and that man could reach this enlightened state naturally, delightfully.

His voice became more audible and fell gently on the ear. The words were strong with authority. There was no thought of doubting what he said. He used many similes and spoke in simple language.

"We do not make an effort to get rid of darkness.
Only shine a bright light and the darkness goes by itself."

The room seemed to fill with light. For a split second I tore myself away from his gaze to see the others. Everyone was enraptured, a hint of a smile on each face, all drinking up his words. And I, too, could not get enough.

He singled out a large, red rose and emphasized a few points with it. As the rose waved back and forth I noticed his hands… definite in movement, strong and beautiful. As I watched, he opened the palm and inclined it gently towards the audience.

Somehow my heart fell into that opened palm.

As he spoke on, I seemed to be aware of knowledge not directly related to what he was saying. Most often thoughts from the New Testament came to mind, fresh, almost new in meaning.

So often he said, "Life is bliss," and when he said it, the desire for bliss, for happiness, rose up strong in me. I was filled with desire.

After a period of quiet the lecture seemed over, and he sat silent again. The air was filled with his words.

I wanted to be still, but the lady next to me spoke.

"Did you enjoy it?"

"Yes, very much."

Now the mood was broken. "Do you know anything about this man?" I asked.

"Oh, yes," she went on, "I met him on the plane coming from Hawaii."

How fascinating to think of him on a plane!

"What was he doing in Hawaii?"

The woman talked on, bringing in personal experiences of how much he had helped her. I wanted to hear all she had to say, but I was also trying to keep hold of the magic of those soft-spoken words.

Somehow I caught the phrase, "...and he is staying in an apartment. It really isn't suitable for what he wants to do. What he needs is a big, old house."

The words "big, old house" rang through my head. What we had was a big, old house—very big and very old—and a bit empty since our two oldest daughters had married.

I pulled at my husband's sleeve.

"Roland, this man needs a house to stay in for a few days. Shall we offer him our home?"

As I heard myself saying it, I was shocked. It hadn't been too long ago that I had decided never again to invite anyone to stay with us. Roland would never stand for this, I thought.

I was in for a surprise.

"It's fine with me, if you want to," he said.

"I'll go get my daughter. I'll be right back," the lady was saying. In a moment we were being introduced to Mrs. Lee, a petite, well dressed woman with unusually large, shining eyes. She took us in tow and soon we stood before the little table, the microphone, the beautiful hands, and the serene face. Still I wanted to see deeper into his eyes, but the lids seemed to cover them. Standing there, we seemed to have little to say. Mrs. Lee chatted quite gaily, as though she had known dark-haired Masters from the East all her life.

"These people would like to invite you to stay at their home, Maharishi."

At this prompting I came to life for a moment.

"Yes, we would. We have a large, old-fashioned home, and we would be happy to have you use it."

"It's quiet," my husband added. "There's usually nobody home all day. Please feel free to use it. It would make us very happy."

The eyes opened just a little and looked slowly into ours.

"That would be very nice," he said.

We stood for a moment.

"Such a wonderful lecture." I tried to make conversation. He smiled a little.

Inside, I moaned. I realized this man had no need of trite phrases.

Now his attention was directed to others who started to come up. Mrs. Lee said she would discuss the particulars with us the next evening, if we were coming to the lecture. Roland and I nodded.

"Certainly, we want to come to all of them."

As we started out the door we realized that we had not paid

anything. We looked around for someone who would take a donation. The man who adjusted the tape recorder went by. We stopped him.

"Doesn't someone want to collect some money for tonight?"

The young man looked startled.

"I guess we should," he said. "Leave something there on the table if you want to."

It was the perfect finish to a glorious evening. Someplace in our busy, materialistic society people were so engrossed in words of wisdom that they forgot completely about money.

This can't be Hollywood, I thought.

On the way home I said to Roland, "You know, I was surprised when you agreed to invite him to our home. I thought for sure you would say no."

Roland smiled. "For some reason I like this man. He appeals to me. I am glad we asked him to stay with us and I am happy he accepted."

"I feel the same way," I said. "Yet, somehow, it all reminds me of sitting in a theater, after the overture has been played, and we are waiting for the curtain to go up."

Chapter Two The Coming...of Silks and Sandals

Waking up the next morning I was in two places at once, my body at home and my mind at the Masquers Club. For me, an unfailing test of merit for theater, lectures or personalities was the early morning reaction. Some recollections quickly left the mind; others left a deeper impression. Certainly the Master from the Far East was not to be forgotten easily.

It was pleasant to lie sleepily and recall the simplicity and sweetness of the lecture. Every moment was a delight to recapture. Such a strange mixture of Hollywood sophistication and the total naturalness of the East! The inner sanctum of the Masquers Club had been invaded by the most natural, innocent person I could imagine, speaking words that could bear not even the slightest relation to other words previously spoken in that same room. Yet these words were filled with more meaning than any in my life of constant searching. The philosophy was deeper than it seemed at first. Yet the delightful way it was presented made it most desirable. And the person! What an unusual personality! I sat up in bed quickly.

"Good heavens, Roland, we invited that man to stay at our home."

Roland stopped tying his tie, looked at me, and laughed. "You mean that Yogi? We surely did. Guess we are in for it now. Of course, if you want to change your mind, you can always manage an excuse."

"Oh, no, no. It's a wonderful idea."

The delight and the shock gave me the needed impetus to get out of bed and get dressed.

Over breakfast, downstairs, I casually mentioned the new development to Tina.

"You will never guess who is coming to stay a few days with us."

"Coming to stay with us a few days? Oh, no, not some more theater people. Remember our bargain? The next time you meet 'interesting' people we are all going to live with them for a change."

I had to laugh. After all, I didn't blame Tina. Most of the guests I had brought home, and the girls, too, for that matter, had been invited to stay for a "few days" and ended up living with us for months.

This, of course, was different!

"I remember the bargain all right, but this time we can't live with him. He comes from India. Besides, Daddy was there and is very happy to have him come."

Tina was a little more interested.

"If Daddy invited him, he must be okay. By any chance is he young and tall?"

I looked at my Tina. A rather tall girl for her 15 years, with plump pink cheeks which always made her seem to be smiling, and, thanks to ballet lessons, a perfect figure. Now how would I ever tell her about Maharishi, his black beard and silk robes?

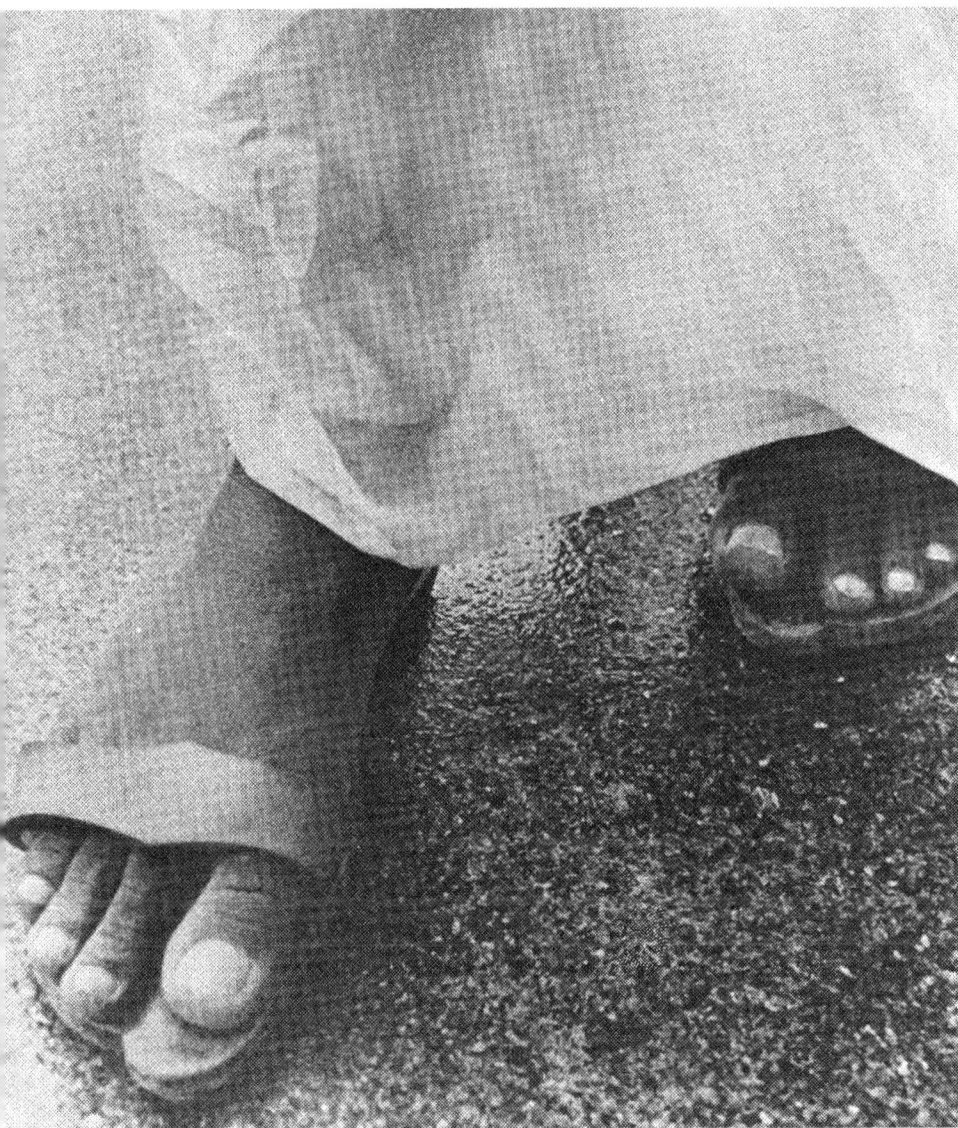

The coming of silks and sandals.

37

"Daddy and I went to his lecture last night."

Tina lost interest immediately.

"Oh, one of those," she said.

"I'm not sure he is one of 'those.' He is so completely different from anyone we have ever seen or heard. He looks like he might have walked out of the pages of the Old Testament or the New, for that matter. Maybe we dreamed it all."

Certainly it was incredible in this day and age to meet a man in silk robes and wooden sandals, carrying roses and speaking so intelligently anywhere, much less at the Masquers Club.

"He is quite real, though," I continued. "He is a Yogi or holy man from the Himalayas. I am not much up on holy men, but I understand they know many things."

Tina thought it over for a moment.

"Then, what in the world is he doing here, and where is he staying now?"

"He is staying over in Hollywood, but it's noisy there, and he needs a very quiet place for whatever it is he teaches. Daddy and I felt our home would be just right for him for a few days. Both Daddy and I acted impulsively—but we liked him at once."

Tina looked at me with a puzzled look on her face.

"There's just no understanding parents," she said and laughed.

Since she was anxious to get on to school, Tina called to Theresa to hurry up, as she dropped her younger sister off at grammar school on her way to Hollywood High School. Theresa, who had been polishing her shoes on the back porch, had heard some of the conversation.

"Mommie, what in the world is a 'Yogi'?"

38

The youngest of four children, Theresa had spent most of her ten years listening to conversations beyond her years. Her simple question startled me, as had many of her questions over the years. My contact with Yogis had begun only the night before, and I wanted to choose my words carefully to describe this one to Theresa.

"Generally, we associate Yogis with India where they are considered holy men. Something like the priests of our church. This Yogi is the first Daddy and I have ever met, and we like him very much. We know you will, too. He looks and dresses quite differently from us. He wears white robes and goes bare-footed with only some wooden sandals that look a little like thongs. Where he lives in India, it is the custom for holy men never to cut their hair, so he has rather long, black hair and a beard. He has a quiet, gentle way of speaking, and he said he can help people to enjoy life more. Daddy and I wanted to know more about him, so we invited him to stay with us for a week." Theresa was very enthusiastic.

"Then I'll get to see him?"

"Of course you will. Daddy and I have invited him to use the front bedroom, but naturally he will have full use of the house."

"When will he be here?" asked Tina as she started out the door.

"I don't know for sure, maybe tomorrow." I finished the rest of the conversation to myself as I usually did when the girls took off.

In the evening my husband and I were anxious to get to the lecture.

Mrs. Lee met us at the door of the Masquers Club.

"We've moved to the basement of the Hollywood Presbyterian Church for the rest of the lectures. It's just a block away. Oh, by the way, a committee would like to come to see your home tomorrow, if it is convenient."

"A committee? Of course, come any time."

On the way to the Presbyterian Church Roland and I laughed.

"Our Yogi from the Himalayas is getting a quick introduction to the modern West. Already he functions with a committee!"

In the basement of the Church about a hundred people were assembled on squeaky, wooden chairs reserved for Sunday School programs. On a small stage were the bench and the deerskin, along with many vases of flowers. The tape recorder was set up and ready to go, and in front of the little bench was a microphone. The microphone bothered me. I said to Roland, "It spoils something to have a microphone in front of him."

"If they didn't have one in a big hall like this, no one could hear him."

As usual, Roland was right. I couldn't help thinking of Kipling and his famous saying, "East is East and West is West, and never the twain shall meet." Here ancient wisdom was combining with modern methods easily. I supposed even Kipling could be wrong and rather hoped he was.

After we were all seated the Master came out accompanied by a fine looking young man. We learned later that his name was Richard Sedlachek. It was Richard who had placed the ad in the newspaper and answered the telephone calls. He was a building contractor and must have found the proceedings a little strange. The Master, Maharishi (Great Teacher), seated himself with slow dignity, glanced at Richard and nodded his head. Richard took one look at the audience, smiled a shy smile, rattled a few papers and started.

"Good evening, ladies and," he turned the page, "gentlemen."

We all adored him from that moment. He looked like a grown-up choir boy with his curly hair and rosy cheeks. He stopped and looked at Maharishi who now sat with head bowed fingering the beads. Nothing to do but go on. Somehow I felt Maharishi gave him a shot of encouragement, but nothing was visible.

Richard picked up a little steam and gave a short history of Maharishi's background. He mentioned how Maharishi started teaching the Transcendental Meditation technique in Madras, India in 1956 after thirteen years of being in silence. After teaching his technique to all types of people for three years and finding it successful, he was now going around the world so all could hear about it. Traveling alone he had come from India, through Burma, Malaysia, Singapore, Hong Kong, Hawaii, San Francisco and was now visiting Los Angeles. Richard's unassuming way affected everyone. We began to feel like a big family at the recital of a favorite son. He did well until he got to the name of Maharishi's teacher, (or spiritual Master), which was quite a lot to say: His Divinity, Swami Brahmananda Saraswati, Jagadguru, Bhagwan Shankaracharya of Jyotir Math. At this point he had everyone's deepest sympathy and got a big round of applause. Maharishi smiled at him as he left the stage.

The group settled down to enjoy the lecture. Again the simple, beautiful words of hope.

"Wandering isn't the nature of the mind. The nature of the mind is to settle down in bliss. It is natural for the mind to enjoy more. Only it needs direction to find the right place. Only a matter of turning within...to the Kingdom of Heaven within, as Lord Christ has said."

Roland and I looked at each other. We were both relieved. We knew, of course, the beautiful words we had heard from this Sage

His Divinity Swami Brahmananda Saraswati,
Jagadguru, Bhagwan Shankaracharya of Jyotir Math

were great truths. But to hear Christ spoken of so naturally and with honor made us very happy. At that time we had not defined Christianity. We had only attempted to understand and practice it. Somehow I knew I would not practice Christianity less for listening to this man, perhaps even more.

"Can a fish remain thirsty in a pond of water? No. Only if he wants to remain thirsty. Otherwise he has only to open the mouth, and the water will be in. Man was not born to suffer. He has no right to suffer. Suffering brings shame to the Almighty Merciful Father. Man has only to know the Kingdom of Heaven within, and all else will be added: all power, all joy, all bliss, all creativity. Almighty Merciful Father has made bliss omnipresent."

Somehow he brought bliss, joy, even the Almighty, Merciful Father into the palm of the hand.

"The Kingdom of Heaven is within me, and 'me' means the 'Me' of everything. The Kingdom of Heaven is within everyone no matter who he is. It is within everything. It is to be enjoyed. Bliss is everywhere. What is needed is only a few minutes morning and evening to go to the treasury, come out and spend in the market place."

A ripple of laughter went through the crowd. The idea had great appeal. Maharishi had the entire audience with him. Although he seemed unfamiliar with our ways, he reacted quickly and so went on more about the market place. Now, the Almighty, Merciful Father became a millionaire.

"If the son of a millionaire is found poor and in rags in the market place, he makes the millionaire suffer. He brings shame to the millionaire when there is no need for him to be poor. All is there for him. Only a matter of turning inward. Man has spent all his time searching for

happiness. In the outer glories of life man has forgotten the inner glories. He cannot spend in the market place if he has not been to the treasury.

And the way is easy, quick, the jet age. No need to take a long time. Only the right technique is needed."

On it went. Sometimes the words rolled with the depth of the ocean and sometimes were wafted through the hall gently as soft breezes. I was not sure what the simple technique was, but I knew I wanted it.

Now he had finished, and many hands were raised for questions. Having no background in metaphysics or yoga I couldn't ask an intelligent question, but I attempted to find out about the simple technique. I couldn't seem to ask properly because he never answered my question, only nodded and smiled.

All evening the beautiful words of Christ in the New Testament had been going through my mind, as they must have for many others, because some of the questions asked were:

"Is this what Christ meant by 'My yoke is light'?"

"Is this the surrender of the Will?"

"Is this Salvation?"

"Can one become one with the Father in physical existence?"

"Is the Bible's New Testament truth or fiction?"

He answered all questions simply but from his own background. He said he had not read the New Testament, but, in answer to the last question, he said, "It is authentic."

No one wanted to go home, but finally we had to leave. We were relieved to see someone had placed a little basket on a table near the door and a piece of cardboard said, "Donations."

Mrs. Lee said the committee would come on Saturday since

the lectures would continue for another week in view of the many inquiries being made.

I was more than ready for them on Saturday. Although our furnishings were not new, the house carried a charm of its own. Fresh flowers were everywhere. All the downstairs was spotless, and the front bedroom was scrubbed. Our bedrooms got a casual going-over but nothing special.

The committee arrived. It consisted of Mr. and Mrs. Lee and Richard Sedlachek and two or three others. We tried to relieve their embarrassment by assuring them we would have done the same thing. They looked through the house quickly.

"People think quite differently in India," said Mrs. Lee, "but I am sure Maharishi will like being here; and the people who come will enjoy being here too. We don't know exactly when he will come."

After they left we sat in the living room. In a short time the phone rang. It was Mr. Lee.

"Maharishi would like to come immediately to see the house. He could be there in ten minutes," he said.

I panicked.

"Tina, get a white sheet quickly. No, make some punch. No, get some more ivy."

"What do you want a white sheet for?" asked Tina. "What's the matter with you? You'd think we never had company before."

"This is different. He always sits on a bench with a deerskin on it, and I think we should cover a chair for him to sit on."

"A deerskin!" Tina was speechless but she got the sheet and fixed it on an armchair. Roland made punch. Suddenly things were happening too soon, and we just sat.

An hour went by. I couldn't seem to sit still. I looked at Theresa. She was pale.

"Let's go outside and walk in front of the house. We might feel better."

Outside, Theresa and I walked up and down. I felt as though I were a violin with the strings drawn too tightly. As we walked up and down on the sidewalk, I couldn't help studying the sky. It was a bright, clear afternoon.

We picked white geraniums that were blooming near the front steps and looked up just in time to see a car park right in front.

Theresa had not yet seen Maharishi, and as he alighted from the car, she started to run toward him. His eyes met hers and both smiled as he commenced a slow, regal walk to our steps. Roland joined us to greet him. Theresa and I presented him the white geraniums.

"Nice," he said.

"Come in," said Roland who escorted him to the sheet-draped armchair. He sat in it in the cross-legged position. Tina came in to meet him, and, as I expected, talked to him casually and easily as we all wished to do. I enjoyed just looking at him.

We offered punch. He declined and asked for water. Tina and Theresa served him. Then we invited him to see the house.

The Siamese cats, Su-Ling and Mei-Ling, came with him from the living room into a small library. Turning into the study, he lingered a moment, then proceeded down the hall to view the dining room, saying nothing. He nodded quite often to the little retinue following. We were hoping he liked it.

When we came to the stairs, Roland asked Maharishi if he

would like to see the room we had prepared for him. He nodded, and we went upstairs. The two cats raced ahead.

The front bedroom was large and airy with windows on two sides. Naturally, it was a little on the dainty side, as it had been decorated for our two oldest daughters while they were home. He stood only at the door. As we went down the small hall to point out the bath, he stood silently. Then he said, "What is there?" motioning to a separate wing of the house.

"Oh, Maharishi," I laughed, "that is Tina's room."

I nodded toward her, and was a little surprised to see a slight frown on her face.

"Even we rarely go in there," I started to say.

"I see it?" came the reply.

I felt trapped.

Every large home and family has a room that gets its door closed when company comes. This room was like that most of the time! We felt Tina's need to be free, and we put as little restriction on her as possible. Her room was completely her private kingdom. Only Su-Ling, Tina's special favorite cat, came and went freely.

Although she had spent the morning cleaning her domain, I had great hesitancy in opening the door. She had always said, "I can't relax when things are too neat."

At this fateful moment we stood in front of the closed door anticipating the worst. I caught Tina's eye as she stood there watching adults invade her world. I wanted to leave the door closed but had to take hold of the knob and open it. Tina's life was to change too.

I heard a deep gasp come from Maharishi as he stepped back.

Every inch of the walls not adorned with doll collections was

47

covered with souvenirs from school proms, menus, pom-poms from ball games, a toreador poster, ballet posters, movie star pictures, a cow bell and other props from the theater.

But the bed was made, and all clothing was put away.

Maharishi's eyes took in the whole collection, and came to rest on the four large windows framed with trees and tropical vines. The curtains blowing free in the afternoon breeze gave the well decorated room an air of seclusion and a suggestion of simplicity.

"If you would like to stay in here, we can take some things off the walls."

He smiled a little.

"That would be very nice."

I thought everything was fine until, out of the corner of my eye, I caught a glimpse of Tina's face. I shut my eyes quickly and ushered the group downstairs to safer ground.

After the family was once again alone, I took Tina in my arms. She was near tears.

"If that man is so holy, he understands how I feel about my room! Nobody can have my bedroom! Why can't he use the front bedroom?" Her eyes glowed like fiery coals.

"I wish he would have, Tina. But, for some reason, he liked your room. I think it is quite an honor."

Tina was not convinced.

We decided on silence as the best defense and started packing the doll collections. It was amazing even to us, but we finally managed to get the room to a degree of order and took a hasty look at the bath.

Although large and old-fashioned, we had done our best to

modernize it and bring it up to date. The girls had chosen a paper for the walls which illustrated fashion models walking poodles.

It wasn't quite what we would have selected for this guest from the quiet Himalayas, but, I thought, at least the models are dressed for the street and those poodles can't get down and bark!

We understood from the committee our home would be needed for about ten days.

My husband and I talked it over again. The only difficulty was my having to maintain my job at the summer theater where I had been responsible for educational and industrial public relations for many years. My contacts with universities and the industry kept me alert, and the entire family was at home backstage and enjoyed the entertainment as often as they cared to come.

The difficulty was the pressure because of the short summer season. Mistakes were disastrous since there was no time to rectify them, and the entire staff became tense and worried. But the theater did not open before the end of May, and I felt I could do the early routine tasks of my work and still be ready for the big activity by the first of June.

Maharishi, it seemed, would be with us from the eighth of May to the fifteenth of May. Certainly within just ten days no serious problems could occur; so we put our minds at rest.

On Tuesday evening, May eighth, an announcement was made at the lecture hall that Maharishi would be staying at 433 South Harvard Boulevard.

My husband and I looked at each other. He was smiling in anticipation. Butterflies were dancing in my stomach.

We listened to another inspiring lecture and lingered in our seats as did many others. Those who had been attending the lectures regularly began to have a bond which deepened as wisdom and laughter were shared.

Although there was never a wasted word in Maharishi's lectures, there was no strain or effort to understand him. Few people ever left the hall before he did. Many wished to say a word or two of greeting. Some expressed appreciation or asked questions. To all he was gracious, gentle, never hurried. Each person who came in his direct contact left smiling and looking content.

Finally we approached his chair, saying, "Maharishi, we are going to take you home with us tonight. Are you ready to go?"
"Yes. Come."

And as he left his chair my husband followed with the deerskin folded over his arm.

We escorted the Master to our car. Richard Sedlachek drove up in a sports car, the same one we and many others had seen Maharishi come and go in a few times. We had enjoyed the sight of a Yogi in a white robe, black beard flying in the breeze, a bouquet of roses in his hands, looking perfectly natural, riding in a Karmann Ghia sports car!

"Here are his things," said Richard to me.

With that comment he gently put a small carpet-roll in my arms. I looked at it—a flower-patterned carpet of exquisite quality tied at each end. It was not so light in weight, however.

How enchanting! Who but such a person as a Master could go around the world with his belongings tied up in a carpet? I thought.

The carpet roll and I settled in the back seat of our car. It is hard to explain how sweet it was to hold the carpet. I started to pat it as one does a new baby in its blankets but stopped this motherly gesture, smiling to myself.

What is the matter with me? I thought. Still I held it tenderly.

In the front seat a normal conversation was in order. Maharishi and my husband were discussing how large a city Los Angeles was, and how much larger it was becoming with the many apartments and tall buildings going up. Soon we were home and in the house.

We escorted our guest to his room. The bed, with crisp white sheets and white blankets, looked inviting, or so we thought.

For no apparent reason Maharishi removed the blankets and untied the carpet roll.

"What is wrong?" Roland and I asked anxiously at the same time.

Then, almost shyly, so as not to hurt our feelings, he said as he drew out exquisite silk sheets, pillow and spread:

"These have been provided for me by the devotees of India."

I had never seen silk sheets before. I looked again at our Yogi, still a quiet, unassuming person in white silk robes who stood there in the room, but something more could be sensed.

As we spread the lovely sheets, I enjoyed every second. The simple bed that had served our children now had the look of royalty. Our guest, as I glanced at him quickly, had the same simplicity and royalty.

He glanced over it as we finished.

"Nice," he said.

"Very nice," we agreed.

I was wondering, Now, what else is in the little carpet roll?

I soon knew for as I started to pick up the blankets for the bed he shook his head, signifying no, and pulled out a dark brown robe resembling a large shawl.

"But, Maharishi, the nights are cold here. That will never be enough."

A lovely joy came to his eyes.

"This will keep me warm," he said.

It was soft and light in weight. Yes, cashmere would indeed keep him warm.

He kept unfolding it until it covered the bed entirely, and the gesture of love which lay spread out before us made us wonder more about this person.

We showed him the closet. He laughed, saying:

"I have no use."

Then he lifted neatly folded silk pieces from the rug, a small metal box of toilet articles, a little clock and a fountain pen, and our Yogi was all unpacked.

Since we had a little ritual of evening prayers within our family, we invited Maharishi to join us.

We gathered in the study. Roland opened with prayers of his own asking for guidance and wisdom. He opened the Bible at random, handed it to Theresa, who read from Mark, Chapter 13, Verses 24–27:

But in those days, after that tribulation, the sun will be darkened, and the moon will not give her light, and the stars of heaven will be falling, and the powers that are in heaven will be shaken. And then they will see the Son of Man coming upon clouds with great power and majesty. And then he will send forth his angels and will gather his elect from the four winds, from the uttermost parts of the earth to the uttermost parts of heaven.

Then we sat in silence. Our little ritual lasted half an hour. When it was over, the Master who now sat with us in our family circle, said, "A good silence, but I will add power to it. I will instruct you in the morning."

With that surprise for us he excused himself and went up to his room.

As we went to bed Roland and I discussed the strangeness of all that seemed to be happening.

"What do you suppose this personal instruction actually is?" I asked.

Roland said, "Maybe we will begin the technique of going to the field of bliss he talks about. I certainly hope so. We have heard enough about it to make our mouths water."

As I grew drowsy, I tried to reach an explanation for our having a holy man from the Himalayas under our roof; and I thought of Tina, tucked away in the front bedroom, still keeping an open eye on her own beloved room; and I thought of Theresa, happy, natural with Maharishi as though she had met a person with whom there existed no barriers.

I closed my eyes, smiling over the antics of the two Siamese cats and intrigued by our newly acquired guest, by far the most interesting and mysterious of any who had come under our roof.

Chapter Three **Out of the Silence —Laughter**

A delicate situation faced us in the morning. Last night our Yogi had said, "I will instruct you in the morning."

Now Roland and I were thinking over this personal instruction.

"What do you suppose we are getting into?" I asked my husband as I looked through my closet to find a suitable dress.

"I don't think it is anything we need to worry about. As far as I can make out from his lectures, he has to give us a certain word to repeat. When we say that word our minds become quiet automatically and we can get to Transcendental Consciousness."

I took another look at Roland. He didn't say much, but he certainly had a way of getting to the center of things with no fuss.

"If it's that simple why doesn't he just whisper the word to us and not bother with a ceremony of instruction? I've had enough ceremony and rituals to last me a lifetime. I don't care about having any more."

"We don't know whether there is any ceremony or not. But, if you don't want to, we don't need to do it."

"Do you think we should wait until we know something more about it or at least talk to someone who has already been instructed?"

All the time I was posing these questions I was dressing as hurriedly and yet as carefully as possible. Inside I felt as though I had a very important date, but somehow it didn't quite add up.

"Perhaps he won't mention it this morning," said Roland. "If he doesn't we will let matters take their own course."

As I heard the soft fall of wooden sandals in the upstairs hall, I ran outside and picked the last few white geraniums. Why? I don't know. I handed a few to Roland who took them automatically. We didn't have a chance to speak. As Maharishi met us in the hall, he smiled and said, "Come."

It is a pity that this word has to be written. In that "Come," spoken so gently, was the strength of velvet. It was the tone of a voice filled with love, speaking to the very core of one's being.

We followed him into the study, with no thought of resistance, and found a different room from the one we had left the night before: pungent incense, small lights, little dishes, candles, a picture of his Master, vases and vases of flowers. They were the flowers we had placed throughout the house. Here they looked so different. Briefly, I wondered who had fixed it all.

No words were spoken, and in the quiet, as we stood with him, something of the world fell away. The essence of wisdom and serenity and purity filled the room. I could not help but think, This man speaks to us through silence.

He had us place our flowers on a small table. Very quickly we were given our technique and told to sit with our eyes closed and practice it in his presence.

In the first few seconds I felt my entire being enlivened, and then a penetrating sensation of warmth, a flood of delight, of love.

After some time, a soft voice whispered, "Open your eyes." Roland and I opened our eyes to look into each other's. I gasped at the sight of Roland's face. It was serene, yet glowing. All the drawn, serious lines seemed erased. His eyes were large and shining. I hoped mine were the same.

Maharishi had fulfilled his promise of bliss.

We sat for a moment, then Roland said, "The word you gave me, does it mean anything at all?"

"No," said Maharishi. "It has no meaning. That is why it can carry you from the conscious level of thought. If you repeat it innocently as a child, you will go within very deep. It is like a boat to carry the mind to bliss."

"What sort of a 'word' is this; is it for Christians?"

Maharishi smiled. "These words were known many, many centuries before there were Christian words, and the effects of saying these words are well known. This is the ancient Vedic tradition that is passed down through our Masters. If you had a Christian word you would associate thoughts, and you would be trapped on the conscious level of thought. My words are just words. They do not belong to any religion. Do you feel happy?"

"Oh, yes, I certainly do. I want to thank you for coming to our home and giving us this blessing," said Roland.

To me, Maharishi said, "How do you feel?"

I laughed a high, little nervous laugh. He seemed puzzled. I wanted to say so much, but I simply could not formulate any questions or define my feelings. In answer I whispered, "Thank you."

As I sat there holding the flower he gave me, I looked up to see a beautiful smile on his face.

"Do this a few minutes regularly morning and evening. We shall discuss it more in the lectures."

Personal instruction was over.

Roland went to work. I always arrived at the theater between eleven and eleven-thirty. I truly had no desire to work on this day. Projects of ticket selling just didn't appeal to me.

Tina, the practical daughter of the Olson family, reminded me that Maharishi had not yet had breakfast.

"Good heavens," I declared, "what do you suppose he eats?"

"He looks like Elias or John the Baptist; wild honey and locusts, no doubt," said Tina, in a matter-of-fact manner.

"Why, Tina, you know about the Bible. Congratulations."

Generally, Tina was not present for prayers in the evening if she could escape, so I was happy to hear her quote anything from the Bible, even if it were wild honey and locusts!

I went into the study. Maharishi was sitting silently, crosslegged on the divan. I believe I would not have spoken, but he raised his head saying, "Hmmm?" which we all soon learned meant, "What is it?"

"What may I serve you for breakfast?"

"Some warm milk with a little honey," was his reply.

Tina did not seem to be so far off after all. As I prepared the milk and honey I picked up one glass after another and promptly discarded it, not satisfied until I held my best crystal in my hand. Ordinarily, I would not have used it for breakfast.

Oh well, I thought, what am I saving it for?

I placed it on a tray topped with one of my best doilies and a linen napkin. The tray still didn't look right; a flower made it better.

Glancing at my offering, I thought, I wonder how people in India who present silk sheets serve him—probably with napkins made from butterfly wings.

He accepted the crystal and the linen quite naturally. I lingered because I now loved the feeling of the study. I was also quite fascinated with the idea of how a heavily bearded man would manage to drink a glass of milk. His manners were most fastidious but not unnatural. Watching him, I realized he wanted water to cleanse his hands. I brought a dampened cloth. He seemed delighted with this small service.

I longed to talk with him but did not know what to say or how to begin.

He broke the awkward silence by saying, "You have to go to office?" I did not recall having mentioned it.

"I rather think I will not go to work while you are here, Maharishi. I am sure I can arrange it."

I paused, then began again, "Besides, someone should be here to care for you. Who will fix your lunch?"

"Your work is not nice?"

"It is very nice. I come and go as I please so long as I produce results. But it's a miserable place. Everyone is tense and we fuss all summer. It's really dreadful. Of course, I enjoy the shows and the artists, but there is much tension. I would rather like to stay home this summer."

Somehow the show going on at home at the moment made the theater, which had formerly been exciting, seem pale and routine.

Maharishi's next words imprinted themselves on my mind with such impact that I have never forgotten them.

"See the job.
Do the job.
Stay out of the misery."

A simple formula, but it has guided me ever since that day, and I have found it invaluable in achieving what I wanted in life. I had never realized how easy it was to "stay out of the misery" if one really wanted to do so; and if one was attending to the job, one did not have time for misery.

I began to see Maharishi in a different light, and the thought occurred to me, I wonder if he needs us so much. Perhaps we are the ones who need him.

The doorbell interrupted. I went to answer it, and there stood a sweet looking girl with two large suitcases. Without waiting for an invitation, she unhesitatingly walked in.

"My name is Sheela Devi. I have come from Hawaii to cook and care for Maharishi."

I felt like saying, "What took you so long," but I didn't think she would appreciate my humor. Instead, I called Tina to greet her. When I mentioned Sheela to Maharishi his eyes lit up.

"A good soul. In Hawaii she cared for me. A very good cook. Also a writer and takes charge of the office. Now you will not have to worry for me."

I wasn't too happy about that. I loved to "worry for him" already, but in the back of my mind lurked a newly familiar phrase, "See the job. Do the job."

Two hours after my personal instruction from Maharishi, I arrived at my office. All the offices were under the theater. Surveying my working surroundings, I was depressed by the gray walls streaked from rain. It was unbearable after the lightness of Maharishi's presence.

I immediately looked for the production manager and asked her if it was possible for my office to be painted. Her loyalty to the theater budget usually meant "No" to everything, and this certainly was no exception.

I wanted so much to stay home. I threatened to quit with so much enthusiasm that she knew for once I meant it. (I had a record at the Greek Theater for threatening to quit!) But I was not to be allowed to leave. I had a feeling I was there because I was not meant to be at home at this time. Quickly, painters were rounded up, and plans for yellow walls and a blue ceiling passed without comment. The good features of my office were unusually thick walls and a tight-fitting door. I turned off the light and began my second experience of the Transcendental Meditation technique.

After a time, I felt delightfully refreshed and seemed to want to devote more attention to my work. Ideas came abundantly all day long and I was not fatigued.

I wondered if the Transcendental Meditation technique could be so effective this soon. It really didn't matter. All that was important to me was that I enjoyed it.

When I arrived home in the evening, I found people moving all through the house. Everyone seemed busy and happy and preoccupied with papers and I didn't know what. From the kitchen came the delicious scent of curry, but my investigation revealed only one thing—it was all fragrance, no substance!

The back porch was laced with silk pieces hung to dry. I recognized the beautiful material from Maharishi's little carpet bag. Sheela came in to start ironing. Sheela was a great worker but not much for talking! I had so many questions to ask. Did she actually like washing and ironing and cooking? She answered, "Yes"; and after a moment added, "for Maharishi."

As I watched her iron so meticulously and painstakingly, I laughed a little and said, "I'm glad you're doing that and not me!" never dreaming that one day soon I, too, would be among the group waiting for a chance to do the same.

Perhaps the effects of the Transcendental Meditation technique that day were still guiding me through the evening, for I happened to go into the study before I entered the living room—and it was a good thing, too!

Maharishi was still sitting on the divan, looking relaxed and very much at home. He greeted me warmly.

"Have you had a nice day, Maharishi?" I inquired.

"Very nice."

"Have you had time to work on your lecture for this evening?"

"I just say. No need to prepare."

I thought of those superb lectures we had heard, each one a jewel of perfection. Maharishi spoke the King's English, softened, however, by the added flavor of his native tongue. The discourses were so simply declared that, bit by bit, the profundity of his words seeped through one's consciousness. The understanding that resulted was natural, unstrained.

I came to earth sharply. The word "lecture" reminded me that they had announced no more lectures were to be held in the Church basement.

"Maharishi, has your committee decided where they will hold the lectures?"

Maharishi quickly arose and stepped into his sandals.

"Come," he said.

As we walked down the hall, Roland came home and exchanged greetings with Maharishi who opened the shuttered doors leading from the front hall into the living room.

We stared with disbelief.

Could this be our living room?

All the big pieces of furniture had been moved back to the far walls, and thirty folding chairs had been set up in their places. There was the tape recorder in readiness, the chair covered with a white sheet, the low table, the many bouquets of flowers—everything but the microphone!

Maharishi stood beaming, surveying the situation. Roland and I went into a subtle form of shock and tried to regain our composure. Maharishi waited. As usual he did not speak.

Eventually a thought came to me: It really can't hurt anything, and we have only to come downstairs to hear a superb talk. Turning to my husband I managed to say, "Isn't this nice? It works out quite well, and it saves us the trip of going out to lectures and," I dropped my voice, hoping to catch Roland's ear only, "it's only for a few days."

"Very nice," said Maharishi.

That evening we all agreed, "Very nice." Everyone felt at home and a feeling of relaxed warmth and gaiety was the mood.

Maharishi had been with us only a few days when the entire character of our home changed. Mornings, the sweet smell of incense came from the study as more instructions took place. More and more bouquets of flowers appeared in every possible location. Huge baskets of fruit left over from the personal instructions sat on every table. People were coming from eight in the morning until late at night. The telephone rang constantly. The two Siamese cats were always under someone's feet. Everyone was always "shushing" everyone else. It was not possible to get near the washing machine. Sheela made a ceremony of the laundry. Our soiled clothes were not allowed even in the same room with Maharishi's towels. Dozens of pots of vegetables were on the kitchen stove and chaos everywhere!

The evening lecture brought fresh, eager, shining faces to hear the words of the Master.

DISCUSSION GROUPS
limited to 20
433 So. Harvard
Los Angeles
DUnkirk 44745
by appointment only
His Holiness
MAHARISHI MAHESH YOGI
From Himalayas, India
Sponsor of Worldwide Spiritual
Regeneration Movement
Will answer questions discuss problems of Mental Tranquility, inner happiness in daily life, self realization, mental development and allied topics.

On Saturday, May 8, 1959, Maharishi moved into our home at
433 South Harvard Boulevard in Los Angeles, California. To inaugurate the event,
this display classified ad appeared on Page 1 of Section 3 of
the Saturday Los Angeles Times.

Following the Oriental custom, people were asked to remove their shoes. Men and women abandoned them gladly, and dozens of pairs of shoes were scattered over the floors, lying wherever they happened to be removed.

It was delightful bedlam, but it was bedlam!

Upstairs, Roland and I were practicing the Transcendental Meditation technique, enjoying it, and yet we were counting the days until it would all be over. As the tenth day dawned, we breathed a sigh of relief.

"Imagine if I had quit my job," I said to my husband. "I'd have gone stark raving mad if I had stayed home in all this confusion. I must say this much, though, Maharishi surely is a very wise person, and it has been a rare privilege to know him. I hope he has enjoyed his stay with us."

Roland smiled a bit wistfully. "It will soon be over," he said.

Quite early in the morning I gathered up all my soiled clothes with a "so there!" attitude and rushed to the washing machine. No, no use! There it was, humming away, filled to the brim with lovely silks.

"I can hold out until tomorrow but no longer," I said to myself. As I went back through the dining room to go upstairs, I met dozens of people, their arms filled with flowers.

"Can you tell me where the lady of the house is?"

"I don't know," I said.

After all, I looked like the maid. My arms were full of soiled clothing; my hair was not combed; I hadn't had my coffee, and the sight of so many smiling, happy people so early in the morning was a little annoying.

In the afternoon I phoned my husband from the theater, and we planned to go out for dinner. When we came home, the lecture had already started.

Maharishi had people get up to give us armchairs. I was suspicious; why, I couldn't guess. Once again in the air were his wonderful words, penetrating words I had never heard before from anyone. From where we sat I could see the delight on faces around us. Mei-Ling and Su-Ling wandered here and there among the guests, courting attention in their best "How grand I am!" attitude. Now and then they jumped into the laps of the non-cat lovers and looked condescendingly into a shocked face. They were the epitome of the haughty tradition of their feline Siamese ancestry.

All eyes centered on Maharishi as he spoke:

"The brain of man is equipped with the ability to experience absolute bliss, absolute happiness, absolute peace, absolute creativity, absolute wisdom.[1] *Absolute field of life can be fathomed and experienced and lived constantly by man. This is the ability, and this is the merciful nature of the Almighty.*

"The ability is there. The field of the absolute Being is there. It is only necessary to begin to experience it. The only one thing to be done is Transcendental Meditation should be added as a part of the daily routine. That is all. And Meditation is not that as is understood in the West.

"In the West meditation is supposed to be just a superficial thing, superficial in the sense that you take a line or a sentence or a thought and think about it.

"Always remaining on the mental thinking level is like trying to

66

explore different avenues of a pond by only swimming on the surface. Fine, there may be found different corners and different avenues on the surface of the pond. Very well, all should be explored, all the unknown should be known.

"But remaining all the time on the conscious level, on the surface of life, on the thinking level of the mind, all the avenues of life will not be explored. Much greater depth is there underneath the waters. Diving is necessary. Coming up is necessary."

Echoes of other conversations in our home seemed to come from the walls. I wanted to shut them out quickly and keep only his words. I had spoken so many words and listened to so many words because I thirsted for the right ones. Here they were, given so freely in the comfort of our own home. I was eager to hear more.

"Transcendental Meditation is that technique which brings our mind from the surface of life to the depth of our Being. The thought waves become more powerful. This is how the thought force becomes more powerful. When the thought force is powerful, the whole life becomes powerful. Whole life is just a play of the mind. If the mind is weak, life is weak, accomplishments are weak, all tragedies are strong.

"If the mind is strong, thought force is strong, accomplishments are greater, tragedies are not found."

When the meeting was over, I thought it was a little strange that no remarks had been made about terminating the lecture series nor any thanks expressed to Maharishi.

As we saw people to the door I felt unusually gay. "Goodbye, goodbye," we said and laughed and were merry.

Soon the house was quiet, and we went to say goodnight to

Maharishi in the study.

"Sit there," he motioned to Roland and me to sit near him. The cats nestled at our feet. Tina came in and joined us. Theresa enjoyed every minute of the goings-on all day, but she especially prized the gifts of offered fruit and came in enjoying one last piece before going to bed.

Gradually, I realized the joy and warmth of the little gathering. Everyone was at ease, chatting about everyday matters. Maharishi was smiling over Tina's account of her day; and then I realized I did not want him to go. This man, foreign in dress and ideas, was like one of the family. We felt so easy with him and he made us so happy. Just his presence in the house was a delight. No, we certainly did not want to part with him.

Roland must have had the same idea. Strangely, we both started to coax Maharishi to stay longer. He looked from one to the other. Theresa was sitting on the floor. She put the fruit down and looked into Maharishi's eyes.

"Oh, please," she said.

"I think it would be a shame for you to go now, Maharishi," I said. "People are just beginning to understand what you can teach them. Oh, don't go, please don't."

"But the people, aren't they too much bother for you?"

"Oh, no, no, no, of course not. I'm not home most of the day. We eat out almost all summer anyway, and when the theater season starts the whole family goes there to help. I believe I can manage. What do you think, Roland?"

Roland looked a little puzzled. He well knew the saying about the woman's privilege of changing her mind. I smiled inwardly as he did the same thing and began to coax Maharishi to stay all summer. From a practical viewpoint he said, "If you really plan to go around the world, you need pamphlets, brochures, all sorts of what we call 'publicity' to help you."

Secretly, we had laughed a little thinking about Maharishi going around the world. How could anyone in such strange dress, with no money, knowing no one, unfamiliar with the names of cities other than the big ones, ever make it around the world?

Tina said very little, but as Maharishi glanced at her she smiled and nodded her head.

For a moment we sat quietly, pleading with our eyes and hearts, waiting for a decision. Suddenly Su-Ling and Mei-Ling meowed almost simultaneously, not an especially pleasant sound, but something about it made Maharishi laugh. We had not heard him laugh heartily before. It was deep laughter, yet sincere and childlike. It was joyous. It was with us, and it seemed personal.

We were just "sitting there," enjoying every moment. We waited until the last few chuckles dwindled away.

"Maharishi, I know your wonderful laughter means that you will stay longer, doesn't it?"

"I had not planned to leave," he said, and again he laughed.

And so did we all. A surprised, delighted laugh.

On the way upstairs my husband and I felt unusually happy. Even the thought of all the inconveniences didn't matter. We realized, a bit vaguely perhaps, that something tremendous was taking place in our lives.

It was like acting a part without reading the script, nothing to do but "play it by ear."

One thing was sure, Maharishi was not "playing it by ear." It was easy to sense a fine mind guiding the events, and it was delightful to be a part of them. Our home had always been a happy, pleasant place, but now it seemed complete since Maharishi was in it.

No longer was he our guest but rather one of the family. It was a lovely, comfortable feeling. It made one not care about tomorrow or the day after tomorrow; only take the present moment and enjoy every delicious part of it.

Chapter Four **Has Anyone Called the President?**

———————•◆•———————

The house had sheltered many families under its wings since 1909, the year of its construction. We often wondered if the other families found it so perfectly suited to their needs as we found it to be for ours, whatever demands were made upon it.

One might have thought it had been planned especially for this lovely summer. Imagine confronting an architect with the problem:

"We will need a house suitable for a family of six—four girls and their friends. In time it will also have to accommodate a Yogi who will receive fifty or more people a day for private interviews. There must be a reception room, an office, places for a dozen or so people to meditate, and adequate bathroom facilities. Naturally, it must be well located near many bus lines, in the heart of the city, but there must be a quiet atmosphere. It must also stay within a reasonable budget."

Impossible as it might sound, the house had all these features.

The study, which had become Maharishi's reception room, was well located in the rear of the house and was entered from a small library on one side and a side hall leading from the front hall on the other. Two large windows gave Maharishi light and fresh air as well as a lovely view of the garden.

Surprising to everyone were the large trees on the grounds: a large oak shaded the front of the house; sycamore, jacaranda (famous in California for a profusion of lavender blooms), flowering peach and lime in the garden brought us shade, fragrance and many song birds.

Maharishi's bedroom was separate from the rest of the upstairs rooms with an especially good view of the garden.

The one thing he lacked was a telephone!

"Would you order an extension phone for the study right away?" I asked my husband when Maharishi had been with us for a short time.

"What would Maharishi want with a phone?" he asked.

"He probably would never use it, but so many people call and ask to talk with him. Generally he sends messages with whoever happens to pass near his room, but now and then he has to go to one of the other rooms to talk. It would be very nice to have a phone in the study."

We had never had one there because this room was supposed to be used for studying.

When Roland went to say "good night" he smiled at Maharishi.

"Tomorrow, you will have your own phone. Would you like that?"

Maharishi's eyes took on an unexpected sparkle.

"Oh, nice. Very nice," he beamed.

Somehow one doesn't associate telephones with a Yogi. We kept picturing him as living in a cave in the Himalayas. At that time we did not know Maharishi spent very little, if any, time in a cave in the mountains.

In the morning, before the telephone man appeared, Maharishi had a little free time, so I asked him a few questions.

"Maharishi, do you really live in a cave in India?"

"Most of the time when I am in Uttar Kashi. But for the last few years I have been going about telling people of this technique of Transcendental Meditation."

"Is it comfortable to stay in a cave?"

Maharishi laughed. "It is very comfortable in the Transcendent."

I knew he was referring to the state of Being, but at this time I did not fully understand the meaning of "Transcendent" other than it should be a state which transcended all others. It became too vague for me to think about.

"But aren't there wild animals in the caves?"

Maharishi was really amused and his laughter was deep and hearty.

"Some wandering monks and sannyasi sit in caves like that, but where I stay, in a small ashram in Uttar Kashi, the cave is like a very small basement under a room. The entrance is through an opening only big enough for one person to enter. Down there is quiet. No sound. Cool in summer. Warm in winter."

"I could never meditate in such a place. I would feel buried alive."

Maharishi looked relieved that I was not planning to be there.

"It is not required," he said. "That is the life for the monk. For the people in the world, they have only to use the sound I give and meditate wherever they are. You can meditate here in your comfortable home."

"What do you do for meals in Uttar Kashi?"

"Food is not always needed, but when I am eating, a man comes from the village and cooks vegetables. I do not break silence by seeing or talking to anyone."

As he spoke, his voice became soft and low; his eyes seemed half closed. We sat silently for a few moments. A soft knock at the door brought the world of activity back into play. He had interviews to go through. I was already late for work.

A sign reading, "Have Turban Will Travel," had been placed over my door at the theater. All my co-workers and the artists had received the benefits of the over-zealous convictions of a convert; good-natured ribbing was to be expected.

It was nice to hear the occasional compliment from the theater director who leaned a bit toward meditation but had his own system. "Whatever you've got there, keep it. It's good for you," he said.

Practicing the Transcendental Meditation technique had aroused a latent sense of duty in me. I seemed to want to accomplish much more than I ever had; and through just a little added effort, I achieved better results. No wonder the director approved of it.

At noon time I telephoned home. A happy voice answered the call. It was Maharishi. He sounded like a child with a new toy. It was a little difficult to keep a conversation going as I didn't really have anything to say, and the sound of his voice made me want to listen to him and not talk at all. Finally he said, "Jai Guru Dev," and hung up.

I had never heard him say that before and wondered what it meant.

The evening lecture reflected Maharishi's happy mood. The living room was packed. Chairs were added to the library and front hall. Many of us sat on the stairway. All could hear even if they could not see.

For the benefit of new people, he repeated the gains possible with the Transcendental Meditation program.[2]

"Desire more. Accomplish more. Live better and longer."

Someone asked how this could be done through the Transcendental Meditation technique.

His reply:

"As the mind experiences the subtle levels of thinking, the breathing becomes softer, more refined. Less oxygen is needed. The body learns to take it easy. Less pressure is on the lungs. Abilities increase. Mind becomes stronger. Frustrations and tensions vanish."

One well-informed "humorist" countered:

"Is it worth increasing our life span? We live in an atomic age and may be blown to bits at any time."

Maharishi became serious. He said:

"If one-tenth of the adult population of the world would practice the Transcendental Meditation program, war would be an impossibility.[3] The waves of peace are so powerful, they overshadow the desire for war. War is created in each individual, not in the government. It is an accumulation of frustration and tension. Heads of governments are not the prime movers of war. They act as the desires of the people dictate."

Many questions were asked and well answered by Maharishi on world peace. After the lecture a group of men discussed it further.

"What we should do," said one young practitioner, "is call the President!"

A few men backed away at this, some women too. A number of young students liked the proposal and took it to Maharishi. He smiled at them and asked them to think more about it.

After all the new people had gone, some of the older meditators sat with him in the study.

"What are those Indian words you have been saying, Maharishi? We aren't sure we hear you just right."

Everyone looked at Mrs. Lutes with gratitude. We all wanted to know but hated to ask. Mrs. Lutes had been helping Maharishi with appointments and seemed very relaxed in his presence.

"Ah, 'Jai Guru Dev,' very simple. It means, 'Hail Divine Teacher.' Nice?"

"Very nice," we all agreed.

Each of us tried out our limited Sanskrit, and sooner or later we all managed some form of the blessing.

"This way we honor all Divine Teachers," said Maharishi.

That evening, instead of saying "Good night," we all said, "Jai Guru Dev." We loved the feeling of it, and soon more and more people around the house began to say it. We pronounced the "Jai" like *Jay*. It became "Hello," "Goodbye," "Thank you," whatever was needed. It was added to letters, greeting cards, all salutations.

It was interesting to hear Maharishi vary the inflection. His "Jai Guru Dev" to children sounded quite different from "Jai Guru Dev" to grown-ups or the family, or to those he had not met before. A touch of humor was added when he tossed his head from side to side and said it in rhythm. On the telephone, he lengthened the vowels and it became a blessing.

A week or so went by before people began to whisper and laugh over all the fun Maharishi was having with the new telephone. From all parts of the world phone calls began coming to him. Burma, Malaysia, Hong Kong, Hawaii and, of course, India were adding new accents to the melee of sound at '433'.

We were used to long distance calls but still attached some importance to them bordering on emergency.

One night, some time after midnight, a call came to Maharishi from India. Since I happened to be up, I answered it and called him. The conversation was in Hindi; but from the rising tones of Maharishi's voice, I thought perhaps all was not well at home.

"Is something wrong, Maharishi?" I asked as he slowly hung up the receiver.

"Ah, Jai Guru Dev," he said as he saw me. "Nothing wrong, very good. Someone has just told me about his practice of Transcendental Meditation. Others in his center are concerned about what I am eating."

I went to my room a little puzzled. Roland, who had retired early, had also heard the phone ring.

"Anything wrong?" he asked.

"Nothing, absolutely nothing. Just a friendly chat from India."

Before I fell asleep, I wondered vaguely how these people had obtained our telephone number.

We understood when the bill came. Conversations must have been going back and forth a few times to other people and places; and, by comparison, our family sprees of thirty or forty dollars looked unimportant. We had never thought of not assuming all the house expenses. So far his costs had been negligible. A few vegetables and a little yogurt were all he required, but this bill put us in a quandary. We were inclined to adopt one of his expressions, "What to do?"

Roland and I talked it over.

"He doesn't handle money. Everything he needs seems to come to him with no effort. I suppose he has no idea of what phone calls cost," Roland reasoned.

"'Maybe you should sit down with him, explain our toll system and how fast charges mount up. He is so gracious, he never hangs up on anyone. He waits for them to say goodbye first."

"I've tried explaining toll charges around here quite often without much luck," Roland looked me squarely in the eye. "But I guess I'd better do something."

Roland's leniency with his family was noticed by everyone. The only lectures we ever received were about toll calls, simply because he thought it useless to pay so much when we were just saying the same things over and over.

"Let's go in and talk about it," I said.

Maharishi was sitting quietly in the study, one hand on the telephone as we entered.

"Ah, Jai Guru Dev, Jai Guru Dev," he greeted us.

"Jai Guru Dev, Maharishi," Roland began. His voice always became a little gruff as he faced an unpleasant task. "I want to talk with you a moment about the phone."

Maharishi patted it lovingly and smiled a huge smile.

"Oh, nice, very nice."

"Well, fine," Roland went on. "We are all glad you use it, but we were wondering if you understand how the billing goes here."

Then he went into tremendous detail about message units, person-to-person calls out of the country, etc. Maharishi seemed to listen. Now and then he said something that sounded like "Ummm." A few times he yawned.

"Why, the President of the United States doesn't get a bill this size."

Roland waved the bill in the air.

For the first time since the beginning of the little session, Maharishi looked interested.

"Has anyone called the President?" he asked brightly.

"Well, no, not exactly. Maharishi, do you think you understand our telephone system?" Roland paused, slightly confused.

"In India, everyone calls the President. That way he knows about everything,"

"I don't think anyone calls the President here. At least I never heard of anyone calling the President. It is even difficult to get a letter to him," continued Roland.

I thought of saying something to back Roland up, but one look at Maharishi's big, brown eyes and I couldn't!

Maharishi's sad look was too much for Roland, too.

"But go ahead and use it all you want," he said.

He started to say, "Watch how long you talk," but stopped. "Oh, well," he finished with a laugh.

Back in our bedroom, my husband and I were heartsick. Why, we didn't know. We felt justified, but something had gone wrong.

"I wish we hadn't bothered him about it," said Roland. "It seems to give him pleasure. No doubt he needs to keep in touch with his TM Centers."

"You didn't tell him not to use it. You just asked him to be careful."

Roland looked at me. He went on, "I still wish I hadn't mentioned it to him."

But, as he remembered the amount of the bill, some of the previous feeling came back.

"It's a whopper of a bill," he said. "We'll pay part of it and ask the group for the rest. But I still wish we hadn't mentioned it."

"Don't feel bad. First thing in the morning I'll go down and coax him to make lots of long distance calls."

It was at least two years later that we realized the true value of the telephone. Through its far-reaching fingers, Maharishi was able to penetrate quickly into all the large cities of the world and give his message to masses of people. The telephone bills began to look minute compared to the tremendous task they accomplished. Swift communication was as useful for our Yogi from the Himalayas as for the business executive, and it proved to be a most economical way to establish a world organization in an incredibly short time.

But this evening wasn't over yet.

"By the way, Roland, the light bill came. It's on your dresser."

I had not opened it. Bills made me nervous.

Roland opened the envelope and let out a scream.

"Oh, no! Just look at this. Look at this bill. Doesn't anyone ever turn out a light around here?"

In a large home close supervision is always needed to keep the electric bill down to a bearable figure. We had been too sleepy lately to stay up until everyone left. I suppose many lights had burned all through the night. I preferred not to know the amount of the bill. I did not look.

"I'll go check the lights now," I said.

I was only halfway down the stairs when I caught a glimpse of white going through the living room.

In his quiet, regal, unhurried way, Maharishi was going from room to room, a graceful finger flicking off each light switch.

Chapter Five At Home—At '433'

Maharishi's lectures were loved by everyone, and meditators came as often as possible. But Su-Ling and Mei-Ling, the Siamese cats, came every night. Like children, they drank up all the attention lavished on them and amused everyone by sprawling as close to Maharishi's feet as possible. He gave them attention but seemed to prefer to keep them at a slight distance. He managed this by waving a rose or whatever flower he was carrying, often tapping them on the head.

Oddly enough, although they had spent years with Tina in her room, they no longer went into that part of the house but instead played a little game with Maharishi through the study windows.

Because he was accustomed to the cold air of the Himalayas, he kept both windows open in the study regardless of the ocean breezes that swept in from the west all summer. One window in the study had no screen since we seldom required it to be opened.

Quite often Maharishi would ask, "What is that plant that smells so fragrant?"

We would answer, "Jasmine." Then he would say, "Jessamine?" We would reply, "No, Maharishi, jasmine. Actually it is called star jasmine." We would pick a few of the waxy, starlike blossoms for him, but again he would say, "Jessamine."

In the fall of 1959, a very fine couple joined the close group of meditators, Jessamine and David Verrill. Jessamine Verrill was a particularly lovely, charming person with large, starry brown eyes. Helen Lutes introduced her to Maharishi.

"Maharishi, here is Jessamine Verrill."

Maharishi looked at her and smiled, "Ah, yes, Jasmine," he said.

Su-Ling and Mei-Ling took turns coming through the open window in the study. With a soft jump they came from the bed of jasmine plants outside, on to the back of the divan where Maharishi sat.

He spoke a soft word to them, and on they went through the house to their own exit on the back porch and back again to the patio and into the window. Once in a while they startled the new people sitting with Maharishi while waiting for the interview given on the day before personal instruction.

In their own way our felines added to the graciousness of '433' because they provided gentle amusement and conversation. Everyone relaxed in their presence and found something to laugh over. Now and then they added a meow or two during the lecture. These naturally went into the recordings of Maharishi's lectures.

It seemed to me their personalities had taken a decided change for the better. If animals reflect the attitudes of people around them, I felt they should improve. On the other hand, perhaps meditation made me tolerate them a little better.[4] While I loved them dearly I felt I had no control over them, and I resented the service they demanded of me.

Su-Ling shattered the peace one lovely afternoon by chasing a bluebird in the yard and catching it. Her nearsightedness made her miss many birds, and it was seldom she was successful. Theresa and I went to rescue the bluebird, who had merely lost a few feathers but not its voice!

We were about to scold Su-Ling when we caught Maharishi's eye from his open window. He looked a bit reproachfully at us.

"Maharishi, this wretched cat would have killed the bluebird if we had not caught her. What am I going to do with her?"

"Nothing," said Maharishi, "that is the nature."

"Why should it be the nature of a cat to kill when it is not hungry?"

"Mother Nature determines all these things, and the little animals cannot help but mind. Like when it is night all birds must sleep."

His eyes twinkled as he went on.

"The nature of man is such that his will is free. He can stay up as late as he pleases and rest in bed in the morning, but little animals and birds must rise at dawn."

I countered, "Siamese cats are so independent, they seldom mind even Mother Nature. They would stay on our beds all day and sleep if I would bring their food to them."

"It is at night that Mother Nature has said to the cat, 'Be awake and meow,' but it is good to obey."

For just a second his eyes pierced mine.

Now, had this whole conversation led to a gentle lecture? Certainly in my own way I was as independent as the lordly Siamese cats. Without understanding why, I thought of something. Although Maharishi stressed doing the technique exactly as he gave it, lately I had been making a few additions.

He couldn't possibly know that, I thought. I have never mentioned it to anyone.

But the thought kept recurring, and I felt I might as well keep the technique just as he gave it in case he did have such a meaning. Also, I developed a little more patience with the cats, trying as they were!

The hundreds of people who came through our doors did not just speak a few words with Maharishi and then quietly vanish as we sometimes secretly hoped they would. They began to live with us. They were always finding our laundry no matter where we tried to hide it. They heard our few personal phone conversations. They knew our daughter Mary and her husband Peter, who lived near UCLA, were not too interested in the Transcendental Meditation program. They were puzzled over the fact that Melinda made her home in Las Vegas, Nevada, a city dependent almost entirely on entertainment. When they heard we had no background in Eastern philosophy or yoga they jokingly said, "How do the Olsons fit in here?"

So often the cats went through the house howling for attention. New people would say, "Are the Olsons too busy to feed their cats?"

All these amusing little aggravations would vanish immediately after twenty minutes' practice of the Transcendental Meditation technique, and we would return to the scene smiling, feeling it was all a lark and hoping it would never end.

One evening Maharishi shocked us all at the lecture. Quite often he checked the experiences of new meditators as they practiced their first session of the Transcendental Meditation technique, then gave help and suggestions through the following lecture. After hearing the experiences, he shook his head slowly and said:

"It is just working in mud."

Suddenly the sun went behind a cloud. Everyone felt depressed. My husband spoke up.

"Is there something we could do to make it better?"

Maharishi sat for a moment, then said, "I need a completely quiet place for personal instruction. The people must not be distracted. The purpose of taking the mind from the conscious level to the Transcendent is disturbed with noise, and the noise cannot be helped with so many people so busy. What to do?"

Many suggestions were offered. A committee was formed to find a more suitable place, a larger home where there would be no noise.

Roland and I sat with our heads on our chests; we felt so low. We could not believe how much we loved this little Yogi, his quiet ways, his beautiful words; and too, in spite of all our inner complaining, we loved sharing these moments with such a good crowd of people.

I looked at them all like a family leaving home. There were so many fine, young and middle-aged, practical men. The women seemed to have more than their share of beauty. Actually, I enjoyed everything tremendously, but had not fully realized it until this moment.

Out in our back garden the children's old playhouse was in the process of becoming a new recreation room. It was an unfinished project left over from last summer. Now, we offered it to Maharishi.

"It would take so little to finish the recreation room," Roland said. "There should be enough lumber around, and we will get windows. The problem will be labor; it is so high."

A fresh wave of enthusiasm raced through the group.

"Let us see the RE-creation room," said Maharishi.

Roland turned on the garden floodlights, and everyone surveyed the house. They scrambled all over it like children. Suggestions came from every corner. Only Richard Sedlachek, who was an excellent builder, was quiet.

Finally, Maharishi took him aside. Richard was not too anxious to get into it, but who could resist getting the great work this Yogi had put so much effort into not only off the ground, but "out of the mud"!

Richard said about three hundred dollars would supply enough materials to finish the house. Roland immediately agreed to the amount. Maharishi, however, would not permit us to spend any more on it.

Various people attending the lecture that evening gave small pledges. These were constantly added to, and the work commenced.

We were nervous over the thought of unskilled labor, remembering a chicken coop from the war days. We spent quite a lot of money on it, but the chickens would not go in it. We had a big lumber bill and a big feed bill, and very few eggs!

But with Richard at the helm, we felt that all would go well and gave our consent.

A good assortment of workmen appeared the next morning, none of them knowing which end of a hammer to pick up, but all full of willingness and enthusiasm. Maharishi could see the entire proceedings from his study window and relished every bit of news on the progress.

Now, when new meditators sitting with him in their first rosy glow of transcendental bliss would sigh and look at him adoringly, he would answer their pleas of being of service by saying "Yes, you can help. Go speak to Richard in the garden."

Out they would go, unmindful of fine dark suits and business appointments, and soon another hammer or saw was heard from. Desire gave ability to the amateurs; and in the evening, after the lecture inside, a delighted group, accompanied by Maharishi, went outside to admire the building efforts.

The third night of the operation my husband and I received a shock. The entire yard was torn up. It looked like an army of giant gophers had been at work digging trenches. One trench went exactly under our flowering peach tree. As I looked sorrowfully at it, I met Maharishi's gaze.

"Do not worry for it. It will be all right."

There was no time for worry.

At that moment we were told two photographers were waiting for us in the front hall. I certainly didn't know what photographers could be doing in our front hall at eleven o'clock at night.

"We'd better go see them," suggested Roland.

Oh, dear, I thought to myself, whoever heard of people starting to work this late. I had hoped to get to bed early; but, if I had, I would have missed one of the most delightful evenings of my life!

The photographers were starting to set up big pieces of equipment.

"We are to take pictures of the Yogi," they explained.

"We didn't order pictures," we protested.

It was no use. The photographers had learned the Transcendental Meditation technique that morning! Whenever a person was instructed, he or she begged Maharishi to accept something more than the usual offering.

Maharishi, as gracious in receiving as in giving, had told these people they might photograph him. Those of us who were close to him were always afraid of exploitation and did our best to prevent it.

This time it was Maharishi who insisted on the pictures. I could hardly believe it. I supposed he would be shocked and probably hold his hand over his face as our Hollywood stars did.

For Maharishi, however, there was no pretense. He did not object to people having pictures of him, and everyone who came to '433' wanted his picture. He sent word from the study for the photographers to come in there. The photographers looked a little surprised, but took the equipment out of the living room.

"We can't do as good a job in here," they said to Maharishi in the study.

Maharishi only smiled at them and sat immobile.

A long, technical conversation ensued over effects, lighting, backdrops, props. It began to sound like a Hollywood production.

The star was enjoying every moment!

"Maharishi, are you sure it is all right for you to do this?" I asked.

"No harm," he said. "People like to have the photos."

Roland was pleased. "He needs pictures for pamphlets and publicity," he said.

"Maharishi, we will have to show you how to say 'cheese' so you will smile," said Mrs. Lutes.

He laughed uproariously over this, and, as always, the laughter was infectious. Soon the whole room was ringing.

The drapes behind him had not been closed for some time and would not respond to the tugging on the cord.

"Never mind, I'll stand here and hold them together," and Mrs. Lutes stood a long time out of camera range, holding the drapes together. Someone brought a large vase of gladioli and put them next to Maharishi.

"Is everything in proper order?" asked Maharishi.

I scrutinized. His silk garments fell in graceful folds about him, but his hair seemed a little out of order. In those times we were not used to so much loose, black hair. Among the gifts left for him had been many hair brushes. Maharishi used to laugh over these, and we passed them on.

"Perhaps you could straighten your hair just a bit."

"You fix," said Maharishi, quite nonchalantly.

Everyone in the room gasped. None of us would even walk too close to him, and certainly we did not touch him, even to hand him a glass! I always put the crystal glass on the table before him, as did all the others.

But, again, he said, "Fix, do it."

I took a deep breath, clasped my hands together, then lightly touched one lock. From then on it was easy. His hair was like strands of pure silk, so delicate, yet so strong and so sure of where it wanted to stay! As I smoothed one side, the other returned to its former state. Some I tried to tuck under the silk. This was a mistake. I had no idea he had so much long hair.

Quickly I put it all back where it was in the first place!

"There, now, it's just fine. You look wonderful."

"Ooooh Kay," said Maharishi.

Again, the room seemed to explode. In such a few weeks our silent, retiring Yogi had bridged the gap from a few carefully selected words to, "OK"! In so many ways he showed us there was to be no gap between us or between all people for that matter.

We accepted his words; he accepted ours with joy, with fun, with a twinkle from the depth of such knowing eyes.

Now we were all ready.

The photographers were suddenly a little reticent.

"What sort of pictures shall we take?" they asked.

"Certainly not 'pose-y' ones. Can you take candid camera type?" we asked.

Quickly, in my mind, I went over Maharishi's activity during a day. Mainly he sat and listened to people and said a few words to them. A smile now and then. A laugh with the family—the big, growing family of affectionate meditators.

"Perhaps we can capture a few moods," I suggested.

"Fine," said the photographers, "Just tell us when."

Thinking back to the hairdressing activity, I looked around for help. The room was crowded with laughing people. They were all so busy enjoying the procedure that they had no thought for techniques.

"Maharishi, these men are going to try to capture some of the various moods we see and enjoy on your face."

"What is moods?"

"A mood is…." I put my hands out to try to explain. "Oh, a sort of expression."

Catching a slightly quizzical look on Maharishi's face, I said to the photographers, "Now!" and the fun was on!

From there it was easy. We would take turns discussing a word or two with him and signal the photographers, so all the effects were natural and subtle. We said funny things to make him laugh, serious things for repose. The photographers relaxed as

Maharishi got into the knack of it, and as with everything else, he was a Master.

He had a suggestion or two for lighting that astounded us. Probably he felt the heat of the large bulbs and suggested moving them to the ceiling. The pictures that followed were the best of the lot.

So many of us loved his face as it was in repose when he sat with us in meditation. We mentioned meditation, and a beautiful picture that has been around the world many times resulted.

"But we enjoy your laughter so much," said another. "And your eyes…can you look up more?"

Maharishi did this easily as it was mentioned, and the photographers were ready.

"Is that all there is to picture making?" asked Maharishi.

"Not usually," said the photographers, starting to take down their equipment. I was wishing they could have taken one more snapshot of Maharishi as he sat wistfully.

"No more?"

"My, Maharishi, if you stay in Hollywood too long, you'll be trying to get in the movies. I think you might even be a ham!"

"What is 'ham'?"

Everyone howled at this.

We were all tired enough and happy enough to stay and laugh all night. But it was two o'clock. We put out some fruit and nuts that had been presented to Maharishi during the day, and soon a gay, laughing group of people poured out of our front door for the "big work day ahead" as Maharishi described it.

Roland and I tumbled into bed each night happy but exhausted.

"Think of some of these people who come every night from the

"We mentioned meditation, and a beautiful picture that has been around the world many times resulted."

Valley and the Beach. Many drive thirty or forty miles each way. They must be averaging about three hours sleep a night."

"I don't know how they do it." My eyes were closing.

"We are all living on excitement," said Roland. "I suppose the day Maharishi leaves, we'll all collapse."

"Oh, dear, that will come sooner than you think. He has promised the people in San Francisco he will come up for a week. They miss him so."

"It may be a good thing," Roland laughed. "We need to get to bed a little earlier." My husband yawned sleepily.

"I wish he didn't have to go. Funny how attached you can get to a person in just a few weeks. I hope the people in San Francisco like him as much as we do."

While comparing notes with the people in San Francisco later, we learned they always said the exact same thing about the people in Los Angeles!

Chapter Six I Never Packed a Rug

In the few weeks Maharishi had been with us, he had been invited out two or three times for overnight jaunts to lecture or to look at property some distance from Los Angeles which people had offered for possible TM Centers.

Each time he set out, I had a battle with the little rug that served him as a suitcase.

For me his things simply would not stay in it no matter how they were arranged. At the last second he always appeared, whisked everything into it, and took off.

I considered myself an expert at regular packing; but, not having had the experience of Boy Scouts in a family of girls, this type of packing was beyond my scope.

On the morning that he was to go to San Francisco, I was determined to manage it. Now it presented a challenge, and I had a few plans of my own as to how to go about it. If plan A failed, I still had plans B, C and D!

In spite of the fact that our charming guest was going off for a week, the day had come in singing. From the guest bath came the sounds of splashing waters and a vibrant voice intoning a Brahman

Chant. It captured the mind and brought smiles even though at heart we felt a little sad.

From both inside and outside the house those who had arrived early came to sit on the stairs and listen. Some remarked that it sounded like a Gregorian Chant. Certainly it took priority over the grand opera, the monologues, and the other strange sounds that our many guests had favored us with over the years. We were sorry when it was over.

The ones who came early to help with the work had their own rewards. They expressed their love by arranging his simple glass of milk on beautiful, flower-decked trays. Many brought their most delicate crystal, and the choice of flowers was carefully made in favor of the freshest blooms and the most delicate in color.

All of us stood in the front hall to greet him as he came downstairs. He was a happy sight in freshly pressed white silk, his black hair shining with drops of water here and there.

The flower that had been placed on his tray began the day in his hands. His beautiful smile and the blessing of "Jai Guru Dev" greeted each one. Soon he was in the study going over appointments for the day like any executive.

"Maharishi, your plane leaves in about an hour. Shall I pack your things?"

"Good," said Maharishi, without looking up.

That gave me about a half hour to triumph over the little rug. I was glad for the excuse of packing to have a reason to go into the bedroom. Already it seemed different from the bedroom Tina had vacated such a short time ago.

Mainly, it carried Maharishi's own feeling of peace and serenity. Sheela, the only person in the house who entered it at this time, explained to us that the vibrations always changed around a Master. From her we found vibrations were the electromagnetic waves that emanate from a person depending on his thoughts and words.

We were not too sure about all this, but the feeling of peace here was something that could be felt, and I was beginning to realize that Sheela had a fortunate spot. She took excellent care of Maharishi and never inflicted her own personality on him. We were all learning many things.

The little rug was already laid out on the bed. I shook my finger at it.

"You might as well give up gracefully."

The pillow, shawls, blanket, silk sheets, fresh silk garments, clock, some papers and the small metal box of toilet articles were spread out on the spare bed. The rug was rather small and soft in texture, but had the regular weave of any rug.

It was amazing to everyone that Maharishi could pack his things in this strange suitcase without any resultant wrinkles.

I made a quick review of my plans to conquer the rug. Plan A was to put everything inside a pillow case and wrap the rug around it instead of placing everything in it singly.

After packing the things two or three different ways in the pillow case, I discarded plan A. It was obvious everything would arrive looking wrinkled!

Plan B called for a little humming to keep confidence up while the larger pieces were packed first and the smaller ones put inside the bigger ones. Here we go.

"Ta, de tum, de tum."

First the blanket and shawls, then the sheets, the silks, next the clock, the little box, and the papers. Two sturdy pieces of cord were on hand to tie the ends.

Feeling I was about to succeed caused a fatal error. The cords were knotted twice so they would not become loose. Now for the test. I held the rug up and shook it.

Out came the clock and the toilet articles.

"See the Job…. Do the Job…. Stay out of the Misery."

I remembered the good advice of a few days ago. All right, the job is simple and is causing me no misery at all.

After all, this is the rug of a Master, and it is my joy to pack it, I think!

Plan C was to open his sheet and put everything into it and wrap the rug around it.

Undoing the strings took a lot of time, and I began to get just a little nervous.

Well, here we go again.

"Tum, de dum, tum de dum."

Aaah! It looked nice and neat. The strings should be secure but not too tight. There was a different feeling about it now. That shows what perseverance can do.

I held it up on one end and shook it.

Nothing fell out.

I turned it the other way and shook it.

Nothing fell out.

"That's more like it," I was saying to myself as my eyes traveled to the little box of toilet articles sitting on the floor.

From force of habit I spoke a bit angrily. Then, "Pardon me," I said to the room in general, hoping the vibrations wouldn't change too much. Undoing the strings was easier this time, but my nerves were tense. I scowled at it.

"You're not a sweet little rug at all!"

Plan D was simply to scoop everything up, toss it all together with no plan, and nonchalantly tie it up!

I shook the rug, a little hard. By now his things looked a bit disorderly.

Maharishi walked in, whisked the rug out of my hands, gathered up his belongings, rolled the whole business up and handed it to me.

I shook it. A little hard. Nothing came out.

He laughed.

I didn't.

"How did you do it?" I asked.

"Easy. Just take it easy. I am used to this. Packing a rug is different from your cases, but you can get more in it."

Laughter was in the air again, and the rug looked better now that it had the Master's touch on it.

Theresa and I drove Maharishi to the airport. He was full of discussion of how fast the Movement was developing and that it must go faster and faster.

"I am already half-way around the world," he said.

He seemed to have no apprehension concerning the other half of the world: the big, busy world of New York, Paris, London, Rome.

"My message is so good, so peaceful; no one can resist it."

Certainly, no one could resist Maharishi once they had the

chance to know him. He mused over the thought that '433' would some day be known all over the world.

Glancing at him out of the corner of my eye, seeing him sitting cross-legged on a deerskin in my car, his lap full of flowers, I couldn't be sure which world was real—the fast-moving one of freeways or the one graced by the presence of this unusual man. I was puzzled, but he seemed to be equally at home in each.

Silks do not have pockets. I was wondering about a few things like tickets, money, and so forth. Inside the airport I asked, "Maharishi, do you have your tickets?"

He nodded. In his hand he held a small folder.

"They sent this from San Francisco," he said.

A round-trip ticket was there. I took it to be validated and put the rug on the scale. The clerk at the desk was quite unconcerned. Evidently many unusual people came his way. He tied a tag on the little rug and pushed it down the slide with the other luggage.

"Oh, please be careful with it!"

I couldn't help speaking out. But it was already through the chute and another person came up to the counter.

Escorting Maharishi to the gate I had another question:

"Excuse me for asking, Maharishi, but do you have some money?"

He looked at me for a moment, then smiled.

"I have no need."

"Oh, my. Of course you will need some money. You might need something. If the people are late meeting you, perhaps you will need a taxi. You can't go without money."

"I never worry for money. Someone will be there."

The topic was closed.

Theresa and I had to wait at the gate. He walked alone to the plane. Commuters to San Francisco rushed past him. Businessmen in well-tailored dark suits, carrying briefcases, concerned with their own affairs, did not seem to see him.

No one thought it unusual for a man wearing white silk robes, with black hair and beard whipping about in the wind, bare feet in sandals, arms full of flowers, to be catching the early morning commuter flight to San Francisco.

Even though we were heartsick over having him gone for even a few days, we enjoyed the sight of him as he gently made his way through the streams of hurrying people. His gait was so regal, so composed. Finally, he stood in the doorway of the plane, waving flowers until the last moment. Theresa's eyes filled with tears.

Arriving home we found '433' quiet and empty. It was the same feeling we had known after big parties or weddings. At least now we had others who shared our lonesomeness.

We sat around but not for long.

"Why don't we paint Maharishi's bedroom?"

The suggestion was received with delight. While we were discussing colors, someone remembered Tina. "What color would she like?"

Tina, who was practicing the Transcendental Meditation technique without saying much about it, had become quite resigned to the front bedroom.

"Whatever color you think Maharishi would like will suit me. Except pink."

We discussed colors with Sheela and a young man named Ron Sheridan who had come, like Sheela, to help do anything Maharishi would ask of him.

Said Sheela, "Apricot color has the best vibrations." Ron agreed. The thought of a lovely, soft apricot color appealed to everyone.

Scurrying around for more help with the painting, we discovered that Maharishi had said, as he left, that he thought the Meditation House in the backyard would be finished by the time he returned home. Those who were not involved in building said, "Yes, it must be done." Those who were doing the building quietly wondered how.

As far as I could see, their biggest success had been in tearing up the yard and making a lot of noise with saws.

"He needs sixteen small rooms, a shrine room, and a dark room where scientists can measure light rays from the glow on the face that comes after practicing the technique. But the slab is only twelve feet by eighteen feet. How can you get that many rooms out of it?" Everyone discussed the problems among themselves.

While they tried to figure out just how to do it, Ron, Sheela and I retreated to the house. Ron stripped the upstairs bedroom, took down curtains, blinds, and removed the hardware. He worked so fast and quietly that he was a pleasure to have around. A young dancer we knew needed money, so we hired him to wash and paint the walls. Roland, Tina, Theresa and I did the woodwork.

Sheela was right about the color. The soft apricot was just perfect.

Renovated blinds and new white curtains made the room simple and yet beautiful. The expense involved was negligible.

Tina gave her approval and informed us that Melinda had invited her to spend a few weeks with her in Melinda's Las Vegas home, and off she went.

Although I was busier every day at the theater, there seemed to be time enough to supervise a thorough cleaning of the house. We had been unable to keep any outside help after Maharishi's arrival. The need for quiet throughout the house, the sight of shoes all over the floor, the mountains of flowers, the voluminous washings and constant cooking seemed to unnerve the cleaning girls.

Grammie, Roland's mother, came a few times, as she did every summer, and put things in order. She adored Maharishi, and was one of the few people who seemed to have no awe of him at all. She was a tiny person who moved like a streak of lightning.

Maharishi would track her down once in a while and say, "Come. Sit down with me."

Grammie would answer: "I haven't got time to be sitting around all day."

Maharishi would throw his head back and laugh. He had Grammie sit still long enough to start practicing the Transcendental Meditation technique. When we asked her about it, she said:

"I can't see anything to sitting around with your eyes closed. I like to be doing things."

Nevertheless, when she began to get the feeling of peace the technique brings, she never missed her morning or evening practice.

At first I had attempted rising early to "brush up" a little. Maharishi always came out of his room and stopped me.

"It is not required that you clean," he would say.

"I'm glad to hear that, Maharishi, but who will do it?"

He never answered but went back to his room. That day new people would come for instruction, and in their gratitude they offered service. They were promptly given cleaning equipment by Ron and Sheela. By the time I came home at night, everything was neat and clean.

Now there were very few people around, and it was a joy to put things in order.

Theresa and I could hardly wait to get to the airport to pick up Maharishi when the week was over. By now we had learned that the presentation of flowers was a customary part of the greeting. As we had been delayed in starting, we had a difficult choice to make—that of arriving late with flowers or arriving on time without flowers.

We decided it would be better to arrive on time and not have Maharishi waiting for us.

While we were waiting for Maharishi's plane to unload, a large group of people came in from Hawaii. A very attractive Chinese lady and gentleman were showered with flowers and carried dozens of leis in their arms.

Emergency threw away my inhibitions. I went over to this lovely lady and apologized for speaking, as I said, "I am meeting a holy man who comes from India, and I have no flowers to present to him. May I buy a lei from you?"

The lady did not seem to understand, but the gentleman smiled broadly, and began putting lei after lei over my arm. I had to stop his generosity. I blessed him for providing our Yogi with such beautiful flowers and ran to present them to Maharishi. Later I learned that this kindly man was a very important political figure in his country.

We went to the baggage stand, and there was the little rolled-up rug among the shiny, chrome-bound pieces of luggage. So, with the rug once again held securely in my arms, and Maharishi garlanded with the array of flowers, we headed for '433'.

Coming home was very nice. Meditators had gathered on the front steps and each in turn showed great love, filling Maharishi's already overflowing arms with more flowers.

Maharishi seemed glad to be back, and he was delighted with his lovely apricot room.

The house settled down to what was now becoming a routine of personal interviews, personal instruction, the evening lectures, and discussions of plans for propagating the Movement.

Theresa delighted in presenting leis to Maharishi.

I always left for work feeling that all was under control at '433', but one afternoon I received a call to come home as soon as possible.

"Nothing to worry about," said a new voice on the phone. "A man is here to see you. He says he'll wait."

"Nothing to worry about" were the words that got me home in record time.

As I pulled into the driveway, I noticed a police car in front of the house. The answer to this puzzle was inside, seated in an armchair, reading a brochure.

"Mrs. Olson?"

A large, nice looking, uniformed individual greeted me.

"Yes, what is the trouble?"

"We are wondering just what is going on around here. A few complaints have come in that you folks are disturbing the peace."

"Really?"

I couldn't believe my ears. How ironic! We were trying to spread a technique of meditation that could bring peace to the entire world. On the other hand, I followed the gaze of the inspector as he looked quizzically at the mountain of shoes, and neat signs posted throughout the house that read, "Silence," "No Smoking," "Office" and "Please Remove Your Shoes."

"This is your home?" he asked.

"Yes."

I tried to be nonchalant about the whole thing. He brought out a few papers.

"Seems your neighbors feel you folks are using all the parking places on the street from early morning until late. You are holding large meetings in a residential area. And you are disturbing the peace."

I nodded my head, remembering the happy groups pouring out of the house every morning around two a.m.

"Anything you want to say?"

For a moment I repeated the little word Maharishi had given me. It gave composure when it was most needed.

"Officer, I didn't realize it, but all these things are true. Naturally, we don't want to cause anyone any difficulty."

I went on to explain a little of how we had met Maharishi, what he taught, how easily we began having people in our home.

"He is only going to be here for a short time, and I am sure we can see we don't disturb anyone."

The officer was most cordial. He held up a little brochure.

"You really believe all this stuff?" he asked.

"Yes, I do. Although it is still quite new to me, I find it interesting, and, so far, it does what it says."

As soon as he was safely in his car, I went in to Maharishi.

"What it is?"

The list of complaints was reviewed.

He looked from me to the other ladies in the room. They nodded their heads.

"It is quite true," they agreed.

"What to do?"

Everyone had suggestions. A hall had to be procured for the next lecture. The ladies who answered the phone said they would ask people to park on the blocks around us. Those who stayed late at night could be reminded to be quiet as they left the premises.

"A friend of mine who teaches ballet has a large room adjoining her studio. If it is empty perhaps she will rent it to us. Shall I call her?"

Maharishi nodded, and I called Miss Frey, a dear friend, and the girls' ballet teacher.

Yes, the studio was available. Miss Frey would be delighted to have a nice group occupy it. I was about to offer her a hundred dollars a month for it when she said she could not accept a cent less than seventy-five! Dear Miss Frey, I shall always love her.

Maharishi arranged to look at the room immediately. It was located on the second story of a rather attractive building. The room was large, bare and in need of paint.

A huge picture window overlooked Sixth Street and Wilshire Boulevard. Although the street noises were bound to be noticed, Maharishi felt it would be satisfactory for a while at least.

Extremely high walls with a wood paneled ceiling and entrance doors of good wood gave a gothic feeling to the room.

The studio had been used for the past twenty-five years by an outstanding voice teacher. One lady who had been looking for a lecture hall said it was the only place she had been where there was no smell of stale cigarette smoke.

The folding chairs were taken over that afternoon and the microphone set up. The lecture was held that night in the new location. When a police car cruised down our street about eight-thirty, he found '433' sitting demurely behind her oak tree...the dignified lady she was expected to be in a quiet, residential district.

Fixing the hall became a project all the meditators adored. It was their own home, and they were anxious to shower their love on it.

Within a week the walls were a beautiful, soft shade of blue. The men constructed a dais for Maharishi's chair. Ladies sewed a beautiful shirred velvet drape to cover the wall behind him. Carpeting covered the previously bare floors. Every evening a new improvement delighted Maharishi. But he shook his head as he looked over the iron folding chairs.

"Must have better chairs," he said. "Very comfortable, soft, with springs, and must have arms to rest on. Should be nice color. No need to suffer for the Divine."

He enjoyed a relaxed, comfortable atmosphere and wanted his beloved students to have the same.

While everyone accepted the thought of such comfortable chairs, no one could quite see how they could be purchased for less than thirty to forty dollars apiece. This, of course, was impossible.

Ron gave everyone a pleasant surprise.

"Fifty comfortable, blue, upholstered chairs with arms have just been delivered to the hall," he announced in the "Office."

Everyone gasped.

"How much?" was the first question.

Ron beamed.

"Four dollars apiece. We heard about a chain shoe store that was changing its decor. They wanted to get rid of these chairs."

In an incredibly short time the painting, carpeting, decorating, and furnishing were done, and with the addition of an enlarged picture of Maharishi's master, Swami Brahmananda Saraswati, (spoken of more often simply as Guru Dev), the hall was ready for dedication.

Almost a hundred people attended and presented a gift to Maharishi. It was a large, beautiful piece of airplane luggage. He was delighted with it. His brown eyes filled with love as he accepted it and met the eye of each individual who sat in the room.

Every day brought many changes, all needed and all good; but this change brought an ache to my heart, and, no doubt, to many others.

We knew large, sturdy chrome-bound luggage was needed to help speed our Sage on his jet flight campaign for Transcendental Meditation.

We just were not ready to part with any symbol of his most unusual personality.

No one ever knew what became of the quaint little rug, but its place in our hearts will always remain, because it helped carry our beloved Sage out of the far-off Himalayas to us in the busy world of the West.

I especially loved the little rug—perhaps because I couldn't conquer it, or perhaps because I remembered the softness from the first time I brought it home.

After all, who would ever pick up a piece of chrome-and-leather luggage and hold it tenderly in their arms?

Chapter Seven **The Family Gathers**

By the middle of June the activity in the theater reached a high pitch. The activity at home was steadily climbing to match it.

Roland and I, in the middle, listened avidly to every word about the Transcendental Meditation program even though the novelty had worn off. Routine practice of the Transcendental Meditation technique was like every other routine and could not bear watching by the doer. Steady practices of anything had never had much appeal for me, but when they help get one through busy days, they have a real value. All that the Transcendental Meditation program really meant at that time was that it strengthened us through the strange situation that we were in.[5]

The philosophy was interesting, but all that really matters to a person is what the effect is in his life. We began to sense subtle changes in our daily life even though we could not pinpoint them.

Close friends amazed us. They constantly remarked on our improvements. We were told that we looked younger, happier, and more relaxed.[6] Some mentioned my voice seemed lower-pitched. All agreed Roland looked less strained and worried[7] although they couldn't understand why he should with so much going on at home! Someone said to me, "When I am around you and Roland, I feel happy."

One change that I was aware of was my shift of values[8] as far as the theater was concerned. I began to realize its purpose was to express the true nature of things, to increase our understanding of the infinite variety of roles in life played by all sorts of individuals.

Good entertainment must say something of lasting value in a subtle way. It should reveal the true nature of things. The Transcendental Meditation program was arousing in me a search for reality and was giving a direct path to it. And, while it explained the theater to me, it also explained "home."

So it was the simple speech, the pleasant, joyous, natural laughter and the draughts of divine wisdom of Maharishi and his reflections in the ever-growing band of meditators that lured me from the land of make-believe and contrived pleasures back to the simple delight of my own home; and it held me because the delight was well spiced with surprises! I could anticipate every action at the theater, but the element of surprise at '433' was beyond comprehension. I no longer spent hours at the theater. I did the necessary work and came home as soon as possible.

Arriving home one evening, we were greeted with more laughter and gaiety than we expected. Somehow, it seemed to quiet down as we joined in. As the usual two a.m. rolled by, everyone left. Maharishi nodded for us to stay in the study.

Happily he said, "Soon my friends will be here from India."

"How very nice. On a little visit are they?" asked Roland.

"Yes, a little visit."

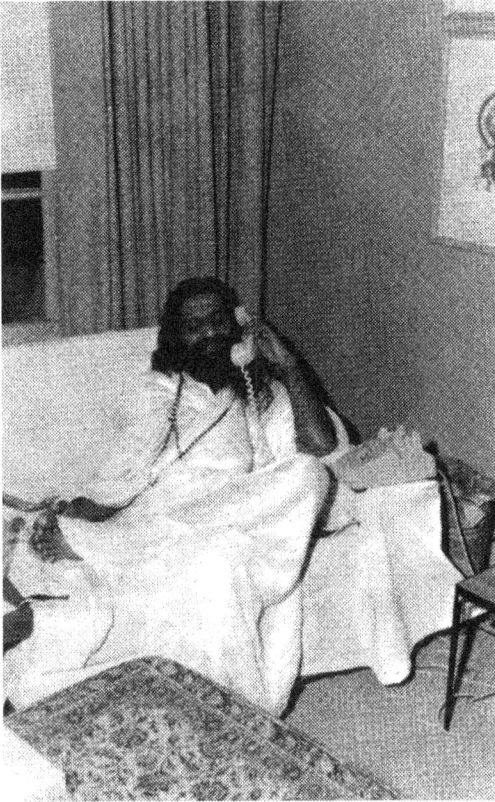

Maharishi spent much time in the study enjoying the telephone.

Something about the laughter we had heard and the look on Maharishi's face made me suspect something.

"Tell us a little about your friends, Maharishi."

"Oh, very nice, devotees from India."

"Are they on a world tour?"

"Mainly, they come to see if I am all right. In India devotees have much devotion to the Master." He laughed a little. "They spend all their time caring for him and serving him."

"That is really lovely. No doubt they will want to stay as close as possible."

"Right. You are quite right." Maharishi's eyes met mine.

"Has someone arranged hotel accommodations?"

"Tonight everyone was saying they should stay here."

Roland and I were dumbfounded. Sitting in a state of blissful shock, we didn't feel a thing for a minute or two. Then we jumped to our feet.

"We would love to have them, but..."

"Fine, very good." And Maharishi yawned his big yawn, meaning, "I'm going to bed."

"But, really, Maharishi," I was determined to finish. "I don't think we can make them very comfortable."

"What it is to make them? Everyone will care for them. Is there room?"

In one minute he was up the stairs, looking over the rooms.

We offered the master bedroom suite we occupied. He dismissed that idea. The front bedroom had been used now and then for overnight guests from the San Francisco Center since Tina was away. It also provided "Siesta" room for the workers at '433'.

"Are they all men, or a couple, or what?" I asked.

"A young lady, her brother and the president of one of the Centers in India."

After consulting back and forth, we decided to move Theresa out of her little room at the head of the stairs back to our dressing room which had once been her nursery.

Maharishi with Ram Rao, Lachsman and Mata-ji,
who came from India to be with him and care for him.

The lady visitor could go in Theresa's bedroom, and the two men
would share the front bedroom. Maharishi had never been so happy!
Bit by bit we realized he must have been quite lonely all along for his
own people, their customs, language and familiar faces. Thinking of
it in that light, we began to feel friendly towards them.

"Maharishi, I am so delighted that your friends are coming and
that we have room."

His smile was worth more than all the extra burdens or discomforts.

"When may we expect them?"

"In two days."

"Two days!" Roland and I said together. After a two-minute silence, I capitulated with, "Oh, well!"

Two days, to him, would have been sufficient time to get anything done. Ordinarily, it would have taken me two days just to think about it. But some of his quick thinking was beginning to brush off on us, and, I rationalized, it might even be better this way—less time to worry.

However, that wasn't all.

"The lady is from one of the wealthiest families in India."

"She is? Why, we could never let her stay in that old sun porch. It wouldn't be appropriate, and that bedroom is a sight. The windows need washing, and the rugs must be cleaned, and the blankets sent out. I am afraid it is impossible."

He dismissed the entire situation with, "What do they care for all that? They will be so grateful to Mother Olson that she will have them here."

The way he said "Mother Olson" fell over me with soft, warm affection. It soothed me, quieted all anxiety. He retreated to his room and we to ours.

My husband and I discussed the situation in our sanctum. Roland, always calm, felt everything would work out all right and didn't take it seriously.

"After all, everyone is here all day to see after them, and Maharishi will enjoy himself so much. He spends all day on that divan. I'd like to know he was getting out a little. As we didn't know they were coming, we can't be expected to have everything "just so." Besides, you have had everyone else here. People from India might be interesting."

I tried to meditate for a while, but spent all the time with my mind arranging furniture and making beds. Finally, I succumbed to the tiredness that was creeping over me. It seemed no time before Mother Nature's little birds were ushering in what promised to be another lovely summer day.

But it was all to the credit of Martha Zweibel that it even had a chance of being a lovely day. After starting the Transcendental Meditation program a week before, Martha had offered her services to Maharishi and was given charge of the Office.

A most attractive and capable woman, Martha seemed tireless and proficient in many fields. She always arrived at eight in the morning, beautifully groomed and ready for whatever the day might bring. Telling Martha of all the new developments turned into fun, and what had seemed to be a problem turned into a challenge easily worked out.

"Call in a cleaning service, Martha. I'll try to buy some new sheets and towels."

Emily Lee had heard my last remark and offered to run home and bring back her linens. I accepted gladly.

It was unheard of for me to go to work at eight-thirty, but now the job had become a refuge, an asylum. I could hardly wait to get there. Driving along, strange thoughts began going through my head. Would anyone in their right mind do what my husband and I were doing? Never!! Here we were, knowing nothing about Yoga or metaphysics, yet supporting it through a complex situation. We approved of Maharishi and all he had to say, even though we approved without fully understanding. Also, the variety of opinions expressed in the house confused us. The people had come from every background.

We knew very little about the Yogi in our home except that we liked him. While we were beginning to feel a little strange in it, he and dozens more were using our home day and night, eating in it, sleeping in it, coming and going freely.

Roland, who always saved the day for me, wasn't questioning anything. Besides, who could tell about this Transcendental Meditation: you reduce sound, and then you come to the field of bliss, a field beyond time, space and relativity. Since it was beyond the field of relativity, nothing could be proved.

...And what does it all add up to?

Three additional guests!

The very idea made me laugh, and wild horses couldn't have dragged my new company away from me!

As I went into the theater I met Coleen Potter, a member of the staff who had been with the theater almost as long as I had. She surprised me by saying, "Whatever it is you're doing, it must be great. Everyone is talking about how well you look and what a terrific job you have been doing. I might try it myself."

"Coleen, you mean it? Come to the lecture tonight. I just know you will like Maharishi, and I am sure he will like you."

Coleen, an excellent writer, was one of the most attractive girls I had ever met. She had a beautiful singing voice and a grand sense of humor. It seemed to mean a great deal to me that such a person out of all the group at the theater would express an interest in the Transcendental Meditation program.

Later, after whipping through mountains of work, I was able to get back home by two o'clock. The front door stood open, but no one seemed to be around. I sauntered in toward the living room and stopped short at the threshold.

It was unrecognizable!

Three or four sheets were strung on wires going the length of the room, and three or four more crossed over the width!

I didn't know what to make of it. Finally, a thought came.

They're drying the laundry.

Emily Lee emerged toward me. "Maharishi found me coming in with the sheets so he had the men put up meditation booths. Isn't that clever?"

"Very clever. What about the sheets for the guests? Remember, three guests arrive tonight."

"Now, don't worry about it. Everything always works out fine for Maharishi. Just take it easy. Meditate."

And she trilled off somewhere. I felt a little unnerved.

Upstairs I found Martha scrubbing the front bedroom. She couldn't get a cleaning service soon enough.

Sheela had all she could do to cook for Maharishi, who often invited others to dinner.

Martha had been taking care of the office and the scrubbing. I tried to make a few jokes. Martha was past joking. "Someone has to wash and iron the silks," she said. "I'm going home for the day. I'm tired."

"I'll find someone or do it myself. Go ahead, Martha, you've done such a wonderful job; no one could ever thank you."

"Maharishi has a way of thanking me." This was her puzzling answer.

Laughter in the study drew me there. Quite a few women were gathered about enjoying the lovely afternoon with Maharishi.

"Ah, Mother Olson, doesn't the busy office miss you?"

"The busy home seems to need me too, Maharishi. Help is needed right away."

In a flash he had people busy at tasks that needed doing. His good humor was infectious. It was impossible to be around him very long without happiness pervading one's being.

"Would you explain to me why you need the sheets strung up in the living room? It doesn't look nice. I don't know what your guests will think."

"We don't worry for it," said Maharishi.

But, slowly and carefully, he told me the problem of teaching in the house.

"So much is lost," he said. "It is impossible for people to sit with others and meditate for the first time."

By example, he showed me how one person would open his eyes slowly to see what others were doing, only to find another pair of eyes opening slowly to look at him. As he did this I had to laugh; another victory for the Yogi!

"Then all shut their eyes, but the experience is lost. So what to do? We hang the sheets, and nobody looks at anyone."

His explanation made it all sound simple and practical. Certainly his entire life was dedicated to the Transcendental Meditation program and to getting all of us accomplishing it properly.

"How is the room coming outside?"

"Very slowly," said Maharishi wistfully. "There is much to do yet."

The plane from India was due in at 10:30 p.m. As Maharishi lectured every evening at the hall and we were busy in the evening, the welcome for our guests was not quite as we planned it.

The ladies had done their utmost in the house. Everything was shining. Fresh flowers were everywhere. The dining room table in the office was cleared, and trays of mints, nuts, fruit, and cookies were set out. Many varieties of ice cream were on hand. Maharishi had mentioned their love of iced foods as these are not too plentiful in India even in the wealthiest families.

Roland and I made it home as fast as possible and arrived just a few seconds before our guests.

A car drove up and what seemed to be three children came out.

Mata-ji was a graceful, unassuming young lady dressed in an exquisite white sari. She wore simple brown sandals. Her black hair was long and fell gently down her back. She wore no makeup.

A very handsome young man dressed in an immaculate white suit seemed to be her brother, Lachsman. Both were rather short in stature and slight in build. But the third addition, Ram Rao, was without a doubt the most slender person I have ever seen. Naturally he would be the one to supervise the unloading of luggage! He came up the walk carrying so many pieces it was impossible to find him! Everyone dashed out to help, but he seemed to enjoy carrying the cargo. He was a fine gentleman, who, thank goodness, spoke English. Mata-ji and her brother spoke only Hindi.

No one had ever seen Maharishi so happy. We had always been entranced with the inflections in his voice, but now, although we could not understand his words, we listened to the tones for meaning. So often he threw his head back and laughed, and we all joined in just for the sheer joy of it.

Roland escorted Ram Rao to the bedrooms. How we wished we could have had the best, most luxurious fittings! Our well-worn furniture and rugs had a relaxing, homelike quality, but that was the most that could be said for them.

Ram Rao supervised the division of baggage. All the women felt an immediate bond with Mata-ji as piece after piece of beautifully matched luggage went into her room, leaving the boys with one case apiece.

After refreshments were served, many of the people went home, but Maharishi ushered our new guests and a few others into the study. Watching the little group all but devour Maharishi with their eyes, and his own eyes brimming with love and joy, we realized better the status of our guest—that he really wasn't "our" guest; he belonged to so many. Especially did he belong to this charming group who had come all the way around the world just to sit with him and enjoy precious moments.

My husband and I began to stand back a little, but Mata-ji kept drawing us closer. She left the room, then returned with a tray of cookies. In answer to our surprised looks, Maharishi explained that Mata-ji's family no doubt had their cooks prepare all the food for their journey. Later Mata-ji showed us the inside of one of her suitcases. It was fitted somewhat like a picnic basket, only with exquisite porcelain dishes instead of plastic. Interesting foods were stored in little jars with tight lids.

It was a lovely sight to see Mata-ji serve Maharishi. The

gracefulness of a lady accustomed to wearing a sari is something to be desired. The pure love in her heart flowed into the offering through her dainty small fingers. She made Roland and me be seated near him, and she served us also. Most of the cookies were delicious, but one surprised me by being filled with hot peppers!

I have never been able to manage pepper, and I nearly choked to death. When I returned to the room after a coughing spasm, Mata-ji looked at me a little coldly. Maharishi said, "She doesn't understand."

"We don't understand" became the keynote of the next few days. East and West had met quickly, and customs from both sides were to be explored.

Ram Rao explained to us that Mata-ji is a title meaning little mother in India. It was a significant title, and Mata-ji was considered by many to be a saint or a very holy lady. Certainly she was well versed in how to care for a Master. She arose early, bathed and dressed in fresh, beautiful saris, meditated and then prepared fresh grape juice for Maharishi.

Her method was to sort over grapes, using only the firmest and freshest. These were washed over and over again, the seeds taken out with her tiny fingers, and the grapes put in a linen cloth and squeezed by hand. Since the process was lengthy, she usually squatted on the floor with everything spread out on a clean towel; but we were forever stumbling over her as she moved from place to place to stay out of our way. It was no use calling for Ram Rao. He explained very quickly that Mata-ji had her own ways and reasons for doing as she did.

Mata-ji was not used to mechanical devices, but she was used to servants. She could not understand our lack of them. Women who came to help out were often quite well off, but they pitched in to do the mopping, washing, ironing, cooking, dishwashing or whatever was needed. It took Mata-ji a little while to understand our middle class society.

The constant service was given in a spirit of fun and laughter. None of the Olson family ever had any of the extra work to do. As a matter of fact, there were often interesting dishes for us to enjoy, and the play picked up momentum with the appearance of such wonderful characters on the stage!

Now that his friends had come, Maharishi settled down to enjoy summertime. Every day the family got bigger. New meditators from various walks of life spent every possible moment with him, hearing his wise counsel, attending his lectures, laughing with him and eventually going sight-seeing with him. Sight-seeing with Maharishi was like an old-fashioned Sunday School picnic; only there was no planning—it just happened.

Many devoted meditators were always with Maharishi. The charm of his person drew men from their appointments and women from social activities. They swarmed to '433' as bees to honey, content to be near even if they could not see him.

Constantly they begged him to take time from his mission to see the city. Finally, Mata-ji showed us how to accomplish this.

One would go to the door of the study and say, with a straight face:

"Maharishi, you have no more appointments for the day. Perhaps you would like to go to your room and rest."

As he seemed to sleep only about two hours a night, he would look like a little boy being sent off to bed. Looking up, he would say, almost mischievously, "Shall we go out somewhere?"

"Yes, if you think you would like to go."

In a few seconds he would go through the house saying, "Come, come." Ironing stopped in the middle of yards of silk, dishes were left, typing ceased and the house emptied. Five or six carloads of happy "children" would set out to explore the Farmers' Market, Disneyland, Marineland, Chinatown, assorted views from the Hollywood hills, drives along the beaches, and, now and then, a drive along the beach at midnight. Maharishi enjoyed the fresh ocean air and made quite a picture as he stood on the sand, soft breezes blowing through his hair and robes.

Although my husband and I were busy at work during many of these trips, we enjoyed the fun of it all through the accounts of Maharishi and Theresa.

Mata-ji began to get a little sunburned, picked up English almost too quickly, learned to eat at drive-ins and commenced shopping for her enormous family in Calcutta.

As more and more people came into the circle with such diversity of ideas and purpose, it became quite evident that with a family numbering many hundreds, some organization would be needed. While no one desired an organization, it seemed the only way to establish unity, and the International Meditation Center of the Spiritual Regeneration Movement began to take form. As a matter of fact, it was born on June 13th, Roland's fiftieth birthday.

Finding Maharishi alone in those days was rare, but once in a while it happened. On one such occasion I asked him about the organization.

"It is a good thing," he said. "I am free to carry on the spiritual

Maharishi visited Disneyland with several meditators.

work. I am not for money and rules and things like that. A board of trustees can see to those things."

A spokesman for the board outlined plans to Maharishi:

"Our purpose will be to make your arrangements for travel, raise funds, procure halls for your lectures and supply you with materials for publicity. Then you will be completely free for your other work."

In India, Malaysia, Burma, Hong Kong, San Francisco, someone always appeared to do those tasks for Maharishi, but now it was no longer a "one-man operation," and many people were given an opportunity to be of service, but coordinated service, through the organization.

The title *Spiritual Regeneration Movement* caused some comment. "Spiritual" in Maharishi's mind meant the highest attainment of consciousness. "Regeneration" meant the restoring of power, rejuvenation, a form of RE-creation. There was not a better word to make known the quick gains of Maharishi's system of Transcendental Meditation which brought peace and power to the individual at one stroke.

Most of the women listened to the plans, heard articles of incorporation written, and were sick at heart, yet they knew it had to be. Everyone seemed to want to crystallize the happy moments of the first days and never let them change, but such is never to be the way.

The reason for International Meditation Centers was to have a focal point where the many tapes of Maharishi's magnificent lectures could be heard while he was elsewhere on tours, and to bring together people who were interested in the Transcendental Meditation program.

Dr. Hislop, a professor of English before he entered the business world, was elected president.

Charlie Lutes, who seemed always to be the one who could be depended on to do any job that needed doing, from chauffeuring Maharishi to building the Meditation House, was vice-president and later became president when Dr. Hislop's work took him away from Los Angeles.

Roland, with his excellent background of accounting examiner at the Telephone Company, was elected Treasurer.

Many fine people helped for a time, then lost interest or had business that took them away. All of the "family" efforts were appreciated deeply by Maharishi who never seemed surprised that people so far from his beloved India, with different backgrounds and ideologies, would put forth such a sincere interest and ability to help him.

A bond of love began flowing through '433'. "Brotherhood of man," "universal love," were familiar and beautiful thoughts; but the reality expressed through the gentle people who heard Maharishi's message and stayed close to him was even more than one expected of fulfillment, and the words "family ties" took on new meaning. Again, words from the New Testament rang in my ears:

"…but who is my family?
Those who hear my words and
act upon them."

Many of us heard his words and acted, and the bonds between us became strong and united us in a big, loving and especially happy family.

Maharishi enjoyed the fresh ocean air. All were delighted with the picture of him as he stood on the sand, soft breezes blowing through hair and robes.

Chapter Eight **Peace and Panic**

———————◆ ● ◆———————

After '433' spread her wings and feathers like a good mother hen and the ever-growing family nestled under her rafters, life could have settled down to a placid routine; but not with a Yogi in the house!

His presence dispersed dullness as light diffuses darkness, and yet one could only think of him as a quiet, seemingly inactive person sitting serenely in the midst of activity.

The summer days could hardly wait to start. Lilting allegros and andantes of early morning bird songs were the overtures to the symphony of the day, a day which might start lightly but often ended dancing a fast fandango!

Stepping lightly were those who lined the tree-shaded walk as early as seven-thirty in the morning, the aspirants who desired personal instruction. Busy traffic came down the street headed for Wilshire Boulevard, but it was not noticed by the men and women who carried fragrant bouquets of freshly picked flowers and baskets of luscious fruits. Businessmen with cancelled appointments, doctors, laborers risking being late to work, housewives, and white-collar men and women were among those who swarmed to '433' almost as though they had been called. All were asked not to eat breakfast, to bring offerings of fruit and flowers, a white handkerchief, and a monetary gift.

Personal instruction was given whether a person donated or not, but all were given the opportunity of presenting an offering. These donations were used entirely to move Maharishi to his next headquarters, to print his pamphlets, and to maintain him until another group could function.

Of all the activities during the summer of 1959, personal instruction was enjoyed the most. Voices were kept low; movements were quiet. An aura of peace seemed to settle on everything and everybody. The big front door at '433' was the portal between two worlds. The sounds of the street—cars, sirens, even the laughter of children at play—were excluded as the aspirant entered '433' and prepared to contact the bliss within.

Each person arranged his gift of flowers and fruit on a tray and carried it with him. Men gave as much attention to their arrangement as did women. The radiance of each tray became a reflection of the beauty and joy of the soul expressing it. It was a communion of nature and man in a brief moment of fulfillment. Full-blown or bud, the flowers spoke of beauty, fragrance, joy and love as they accompanied the seeker during his private moments with Maharishi.

On the first of August, during the late afternoon, the first ceremony of personal instruction was performed in the REcreation House. Morning appointments were going on as usual in the house and proceeding smoothly.

Martha moved quietly and was ably assisted by numerous others.

By noon, new meditators had their first experience of the deep dive within, had been checked for results, and had left the house with their feelings of exaltation mirrored in their shining eyes. The house guests and office staff were invited out to lunch and for the afternoon. Maharishi remained in silence after instructing.

On this day, the peace that permeated the atmosphere could almost be appreciated through the senses. It seemed that one could breathe it in, and let it go through the body. Also, it seemed we were waiting for something....

During these days '433' seldom closed its front door, but on this day it seemed quite right that it should be closed, possibly because no staff was on hand to greet those who customarily walked in. I had picked this day to work at home, and the sound of the front bell was a little startling to me since I had not heard it for some time. I opened the door to meet Mr. H—— and his secretary.

His secretary, a young man, introduced Mr. H—— and himself to me. I was not at this time familiar with this gentleman's literature or lectures, nor did I know that there was an appointment for the afternoon, but Maharishi seemed to be expecting him.

The greeting was one of loving recognition, and the two were left in the little study to enjoy a chat in the afternoon. The secretary excused himself and departed. The house belonged to Maharishi and Mr. H——. An hour was theirs in quiet, but the telephone permitted no more. An urgent call forced me to interrupt them. After Maharishi completed the call, he said:

"Mr. H—— is the first person to be instructed in the new Meditation House."

I knew he meant right away. Looking at Mr. H——, at his lean, ascetic face which acknowledged many years of life, the face of a scholar and teacher, I was puzzled. It was a countenance which showed spiritual fulfillment, but his eyes expressed fatigue. Much depth was in the serious face; but childlike joy, something of the bliss we saw constantly, was lacking.

It took only a few moments to gather the simple accoutrements for the ceremony and to prepare the Meditation House.

The floor of the little house had been completely covered with an inexpensive but attractive apricot-colored carpet. The personal instruction room was encased in glass in the center, and around the sides were many small private cubicles.

Meditators had often talked of appropriate ceremonies for the opening of the Meditation House. It was to be an occasion marked by a celebration, but the reality was nicer. The little room was new and silent as the dawn and ready to receive an aspirant who carried his own light, his own adornment.

As spirals of incense rose, I could see Maharishi escorting Mr. H—— through the garden, a gesture I had never seen before. Aspirants always wait for a Master, and the time spent in waiting is significant. Mr. H—— was not required to wait.

While personal instruction was taking place, the doorbell rang again. This time it was a photographer who seemed to have an appointment to take pictures of the Meditation House for a news article. There is always something about photographers that makes me nervous. Perhaps it is the "moment of truth" they record on film. Certainly the Meditation House was not ready for its picture, and, having been in a similar circumstance many times myself, I tried to think of something else that could be photographed;

but all I seemed to be able think of was that Maharishi would like refreshments served to Mr. H—— afterwards.

"Would you mind very much putting all your equipment down and giving me a hand? Instead of pictures of the Meditation House we are going to have pictures of two gentlemen in the garden. If we set up a tea table it will make a nice background, and also it will give them something to do."

The photographer was good-natured and willing. Refreshments could not be served in the dining room because it had become an office in every sense of the word. The dining table was literally covered with typewriters, files, appointment books and stationery. A large folding picnic table was a good substitute and just right for the garden.

The photographer showed good home training as he carefully carried out pitchers of fruit juice and a tray with glasses and silver.

I followed with linen and Dresden fruit plates. While Maharishi's own tastes were simple, he had an eye for loveliness in ideas, people and things. I knew he would want beauty for Mr. H——.

It took just a few minutes to make a beautiful flower arrangement. The house was filled with vases of roses, orchids, camellias, carnations, stock, asters and many, many others. Baskets of luscious fruits, cookies, nuts, candies or sweetmeats, as Maharishi called them, were always in the house because people never called on Maharishi empty-handed. Very soon the table expressed warm hospitality.

"I certainly didn't know these things could be put together as fast as this," said the puzzled photographer.

"Believe me, they aren't usually! It takes a Yogi from the caves in the Himalayas to light a few fires within you before you can move this fast!"

Just as he was about to take a picture of the table, the two men emerged from the Meditation House. Maharishi looked enraptured. As for Mr. H——, his face was illumined. Now his blue eyes were shining with the light we saw so often on new meditators. In less than half an hour his face seemed to have become younger, less lined. A smile replaced the serious mien he had worn previously.

Maharishi's appreciative eyes glanced over the tea table. Mr. H—— had been instructed without bringing the customary fruit and flowers. Maharishi's hand reached for the loveliest flower, the most beautiful fruit, and placed them in Mr. H——'s hands. Sensing that this was a most unusual occasion, I quietly asked the photographer to take a picture of the two men. Both were talking and did not notice; but as a flash was used they glanced up, and Maharishi seemed a bit displeased.

"This picture will probably not come out, Maharishi. Shall we take another?"

Very gently Maharishi said, "I do not think Rishi H—— cares to have his picture taken."

I was a little late perhaps, but I became aware of Mr. H——'s desire to stay in solitude and excused myself.

The two gentlemen went back into the house while the photographer and I went into the Meditation House to take pictures. The small room in the center remained closed, but a few shots were taken of the enclosed booths where many students were to come from now on to sit quietly and undisturbed. After the busy, laughing days of hammering, sawing, and painting, the house now had a soft tranquility. In such a few moments it had become a quiet haven, a refuge from the world.

After the photographer left I lingered in the little house. It was there I realized Maharishi had called Mr. H—— "Rishi." In discussing the significance of Maharishi's name previously, it was disclosed that Rishi meant a sage, a very wise man. It seemed so right for the gentleman with the lean ascetic face, and the now

Maharishi in the personal instruction room of the Meditation House.

shining blue eyes to be called "Rishi." Whatever was the significance of that day I do not know, as I have never seen Mr. H—— since, but I have always felt it was a great privilege to have been near and to have witnessed that rare occasion.

An unusual day this one was in more ways than one. The peace was in the afternoon, ushered in with Mr. H——.

The panic came that night!

Opening night at a theater is always a time of high excitement and fun. All routine jobs are finished (or should be); the background has been provided, and now it is entirely up to the performer to show whether his art is complete enough to satisfy the public taste. Now there is only the pleasure of art presented in a simple, entertaining form, and joy is brought up in the consciousness of the listeners.

Besides the job of promotion, the "Kitchen" was one of my projects. I had opened a creaky door to an unused kitchen at the theater one day and found an old stove, refrigerator, etc. This started me making sandwiches for the hungry dancers who could never get out of the theater after rehearsal. They were so grateful that they consumed huge quantities of sandwiches, cheese, coffee, fruit juices, ice cream and whatever we could fix. They waited on themselves and left money in the till; but they spread the word too thoroughly, and we ended up having to feed musicians, ushers, staff and friends.

The geniality of the informal kitchen drew all the performers, and wonderful evening conversation resulted. Artists ran down miles of corridors to get a cup of coffee between numbers, and the stars were no exception. This particular evening it was Mr. Harry Belafonte who took the spotlight.

The possibility of seeing Mr. Belafonte in person brought us mobs of volunteer help. Roland was on hand as always. The tiny kitchen overflowed with as many people as could crowd in. Since I had begun spending so much time in the kitchen, the director had a phone put in, and I took many ticket orders for group parties with one hand and made sandwiches with the other! The director enjoyed the kitchen himself and was glad to have a place where everyone could take a few minutes to relax and talk shop.

On this particular evening it was a wild place. Musicians were warming up next door; no one could be heard without screaming; everyone seemed to be starved; and, for the first time that I could recall, I had no desire at all for any of it and couldn't escape. I longed for the quiet of the Meditation House.

In the midst of the confusion the phone began ringing. We were too busy to answer it. Actually, quite often one of the artists would answer for me, take ticket orders for his own show, and the buyer would never dream he had been talking to one of the stars!

Tonight, one of the older musicians answered. Some had enough experience by this time to talk quite intelligently on the business of selling tickets or get rid of people who wanted passes. This time he elbowed his way over to us and nervously said:

"Mr. Olson, it's a call from your home. I think you had better take it."

I watched as Roland talked, saw his face pale and his hands shake a little. Luckily, the bell for the first curtain rang, and the kitchen began to clear a little.

"We will have to go home. The house is flooded from a broken water hose on the washing machine. The furnaces may explode. They keep going off and on."

It seemed difficult for Roland to find the proper words to tell me of our predicament.

I made arrangements to leave. Roland phoned for the emergency services of the Fire Department, Police Department and the Water Department. The person who phoned us was a man who had returned to our home for some papers which he had forgotten to take to the evening meeting. He was to stand by until help came. The Water Department had to turn off the water at the street hydrant; the Gas Company was necessary for the furnace, and the Fire Department was needed in case neither of the others made it in time.

We had special parking privileges at the theater, or we could not have left the grounds at all. Traffic was terribly snarled with cars parked everywhere.

As it was, it seemed an eternity to me before we drove up to '433'.

It looked like a disaster area! Men with helmets were running about, hoses were stretched along the lawn, trucks with routine radio broadcasts blaring lined the streets. Dozens of people were going in and out of the house. Roland went inside and came back as quickly as he could.

"Everything is under control. The furnaces are disconnected and the water has been turned off."

Everyone he called had arrived within minutes. Even so, water had soaked into the carpets; and the three large furnaces were out of commission as was the washing machine that had started the whole thing. When the utility services left, with our profound thanks, we were too overcome to do anything more than survey the situation.

It was too big a disaster to weep over. We walked through the water-soaked rooms not quite knowing what to do. The linoleum in the kitchen and back porch consisted of squares we had laid ourselves; now they all were curling at the edges. In the hall outside Maharishi's study, there was wall-to-wall carpeting. We stepped on it and water oozed up. The living room, thank goodness, was untouched.

Roland and I sat down and had little to say.

"What will we do?" I finally asked.

"The best we can. I suppose we had better start mopping up water."

Our funds had never been lower. We had a houseful of guests who did voluminous washings and needed a washing machine. At times we had secret thoughts that they were all perfect strangers who were in our home more than we were at the time. But, because of a man who met all of our requirements for perfection, a Yogi who showed us a path that answered our needs before we were even aware of them, we had to stand it. Somehow we knew we had to give a great deal to compensate for the blessings we were receiving.

At that moment our minds were too dull with fatigue and worry to think much about blessings. The practical side of life was uppermost.

We began mopping up!

The sound of laughter outside the house told us the meeting was over and the house would be full of people again. No doubt strangers would be added to the group just as they were every evening, and they would wonder about the confusion. Roland and I went to the door and directed the group through the library to the study. The gaiety of the group was the same as always. Little notice was taken of the disaster. Minds in tune with divine inspiration never seem to be disturbed by mundane affairs.

Someone said, "Oh, you've had a little trouble? What a shame."

Maharishi went straight to the study through the library, but for a brief second his eyes sent a look of compassion our way. Of course there was really nothing anyone could do. We were still busy wringing our mops when someone came to the kitchen and said, "Maharishi would like you to join the others in the study."

We decided we might as well. We were getting nowhere cleaning up. On the way we met Mata-ji.

"Maharishi's grape juice?" she asked gently.

I had a vision of Mata-ji sitting on the kitchen floor (as it was now) squeezing grapes and couldn't help but laugh.

"No, Mata-ji, no grape juice tonight. Maybe the health food store is still open. We'll send someone for bottled juice," I said.

Discussions were lively in the study. Some young scientists had joined the group and were giving their reasons for considering the Transcendental Meditation technique a mystical experience rather than a scientific one.

Maharishi felt his technique was scientific and wished to prove it. It was arranged for a doctor to come and make an electrocardiogram of a person practicing the Transcendental Meditation technique to see if the heart slowed as it was supposed to do. Roland and I were fascinated and forgot a little of our difficulties. (The electrocardiogram subsequently showed that heart action became regular during the Transcendental Meditation technique.)

When there was a lull in the conversation Maharishi looked at us.

"What it is?" he said.

All I needed to hear was, "What it is?" and I felt like a child who has had a bad bump soothed. Maharishi could not seem to say, "What is it?" And I hope he never will.

Roland related a few of our woes, but the tone of his voice told me he was not quite as upset over the situation as he had been. After a little more discussion, everyone offered sympathy which we no longer seemed to need.

Later, upstairs in our bedroom, Roland got some papers out of his file and began reading.

"What do you know," he said. "Our insurance covers all water damage. Imagine that. After all these years the insurance company is going to pay us something. What a relief!"

We slept very well that night.

Our insurance agent was superb. He came as soon as we called and took over. It was then that we found out how blessed we really were. The furnace repair people said our old furnaces were in such a state that they might have blown up at any time. We always had them checked every year but not taken apart. The linoleum we laid on the floor was not tight enough under the sink and the flooring underneath would not have dried out properly. The carpet in the hall certainly needed a good cleaning which it soon received.

What had seemed like sheer holocaust began to look like a piece of good luck. It was great fun to look over linoleum samples and pick out what I liked, instead of what I could afford.

I had always ignored things like furnaces and basements, but since they could have ruined our lives, I thought it was about time I got acquainted. The service men looked and acted like interns in a hospital. They informed us of their progress, and finally we were happy to hear that the furnaces (thirty years old) had recovered from their operation and were pronounced out of danger for another ten years.

After a few trying days, we had beautiful new linoleum in our kitchen and back porch. The carpets looked new again. The furnaces worked better than they ever had.

As for the faithful old washing machine, it took very little to replace the guilty hoses, and it soon went back to its gurgling, filled with loads of precious silks.

There was a little blessing in it for Maharishi too.

He was really tired of grape juice but could never refuse drinking it if Mata-ji brought it to him. As she couldn't get into the kitchen for a while, she had resorted to bottled apple juice and other juices with which she had not been familiar. As soon as she decided they were proper for Maharishi to drink, he thoroughly enjoyed the variety, and we were relieved of the worry about stumbling over her on the floor!

And '433' settled back to more days of peace, after having survived panic, which, when viewed in retrospect, made us realize and start to appreciate the serenity and strength we had found.

Chapter Nine **Of Toes and Roses**

—•◆•—

*"The time has come
The Walrus said,
To speak of many things,
Of shoes and ships and sealing wax,
Of cabbages and Kings."*

—*Alice in Wonderland*

"To speak of many things" out of the ordinary realm of experience in the summer of 1959 gives the "toes and roses" of the Master top billing. Leaving his sandals behind as he entered a room, he sat cross-legged and so put the beautiful feet very much in evidence. To those who took a few moments out of time to enjoy the personality of Maharishi, there came constant delight because of his charm and naturalness.

As a matter of fact Maharishi was fast becoming a sought-after celebrity. Already it was a little difficult to remember the shy, quiet, small man who rarely spoke above a whisper. The recluse from the Himalayas, who seemingly had sat motionless on the couch in the study hour after hour, day after day, listening patiently to the woes of humanity, began to blossom in the warmth of the California sunshine.

He began to understand and enjoy the customs and language of informal Westerners, and to adopt a few phrases. "OK" began to be heard in the formal British-Indian speech, and it always brought a smile to the listeners. Bathed in the constant flow of love from every person who came within his radius, Maharishi laughed and chatted with all. Especially did he enjoy matching wits and exploring all avenues of thought with students, doctors and men of science. We dreaded to see the little old ladies who came to drop their long tales of woe on him or sick and ill-adjusted souls who had already traveled from teacher to teacher come to take his time. After he gave them an hour or so we would say, "Maharishi, how can you stand to listen to so much trouble?"

He would say quite simply, "They need."

He shared each day with the hundreds of people who came through our study with their shoes off! Understanding or not understanding why seemed to make no difference. No one objected, although some business and professional men looked a bit surprised.

It was customary for as many as twenty or more people at a time to fill chairs (and share them with people they had not met before but who were no longer strangers) and keep making room for those who delighted in sitting on the floor. Our family enjoyed the floor. Conversation was general. Usually it centered on the Transcendental Meditation program and people who should be told about it. It seemed to bother some people that we were receiving pieces of wisdom from a man from India, since from our viewpoint America was a more progressive country than India.

"Maharishi, we understand so little of India," asked Arthur Granville, a practical, analytical man. "Is education quite general?"

"No," answered Maharishi, "it is as scarce in India as it is in any other part of the world." And he raised his head and smiled. The room burst into laughter. Quite a lot went through the minds of those present. All could feel within themselves the true meaning of education. Gradually the laughter subsided into silence and then he said:

"Our technique of Transcendental Meditation will give a meaning to education all over the world."

Someone said, "Is our education meaningless, Maharishi?"

"It is not meaningless. Only it lacks completion. Education should be such that it develops the full man. Education today fails to develop man's full potential. It fills the conscious mind with information on serious subjects but fails to unfold the subconscious and real inner content lying in the depth of one's consciousness. Transcendental Meditation will bring fulfillment to education." [9]

Almost every day as soon as personal instruction, checking, interviews and lunch were over, Maharishi gave freely of his time to all those who came to sit with him. He would listen to everyone intently, ask a few simple questions and slowly draw the listener into the magic circle of his warmth. Then, little by little he would bring the student, housewife, businessman, the artist, the laborer, to the subject of Transcendental Meditation.

Living in the world of the theater I was familiar with excellent, professional performance and achievement, and, after having seen Maharishi's performance, I was positive this was not just a simple, unknowing person. He was indeed a polished, professional performer if I ever saw one!

The questions constantly returned to his background, his childhood life and on to the present time.

Some asked questions about his home, and generally the answers were simple and direct. He was born into a good family, a cultured environment, which was obvious from his every action. When he had been with us for but a short time I asked him, "Maharishi, would you like me to send a note to your mother? I should like to let her know how much we enjoy having you with us, and that you are well."

Without an upward glance he said, "Mother knows son is doing well."

Doing well indeed! I thought. Fifty to sixty people attended his lectures every evening during the week, with a hundred or more over the weekends.

As we sat with him in the study, we observed the people more and more. It was a great joy to see natural beauty begin to shine through the accumulated habits and customs and inhibitions which people seem to acquire in the activity of the world. A beautiful transformation took place.

'433' was blessed not only by the presence of a Master but by the hundreds of people who expressed love, joy, and humility in their thinking and in their actions. Laughter was our language, and love was truly the universal bond within our home. World topics were good-naturedly tossed about like rubber balls. Everyone contributed his share in ideas and in service.

The hundreds of meditators who spent every possible free hour of the summer of 1959 at our home had one thought—one purpose in mind—*Maharishi.* They wanted to see him, be with him, talk about him, and ask questions about him. Now and then someone would ask us Maharishi's age. I had no idea or desire to know. It always seemed to me that he was beyond the expression of time and age. But, in order to answer other people's questions, I began to scrutinize him.

Maharishi was short in stature, about five feet three or four inches. One first noticed the large, luminous, dark eyes. The face was soft in outline, unlined, youthful in appearance, but it expressed authority and was completely framed in black, wavy hair. His hair fell naturally about his face, blending with that of his beard. His body, draped with yards and yards of white silk, offered a regal appearance. Most in evidence were his beautiful hands and feet. His hands were expressive and strong. His feet were small but well formed.

No picture of Maharishi is complete without flowers since they are a part of him. From early morning until late at night flowers were presented by every one who came to him, perhaps a single rose, perhaps a large bouquet. No one left his presence without receiving a flower to take along. Joy was both given and received, but in his hands flowers seemed to bloom rather than fade. On his person they seemed to come alive and reminded us somehow of happy children.

Quite often we would enjoy remarks made by some of the newer people, "The flowers he holds seem to grow fresher and deeper in color the longer he holds them."

Or from other lips, "It's a strange thing to say, but the flowers look as if they enjoy being in his hands."

Every evening at eight o'clock he went to the Transcendental Meditation Center for the lecture. Flowers were gathered up daily at '433' and taken to the hall, and Maharishi always arrived carrying a large bouquet. He made a picture quite different from that of the ordinary lecturer and much more charming! It is delightful to recall his lectures and the play of flowers.

Flowers were constantly referred to in his lectures in illustrating various points. Most often he had beautiful, long-stemmed red roses which he would touch against the blackboard to emphasize a particular point. Sometimes the touch was not so light if he wished to stress an important aspect of the Transcendental Meditation technique. At the lecture hall one followed the trend of his thinking with the mind, but the eyes followed the entrancing movements of the flowers in his hands.

Maharishi was often asked about the value of meditating on something: many people meditated on a symbol, an affirmation, a verse from the Bible, or a thought.

Maharishi explained:

"Transcendental Meditation is a march from the gross to the subtle fields of creation. One man meditates through the right medium, and he produces life-supporting influences through the whole of creation by virtue of a right vibration. And, as we know, if we hit this flower against someone, it might hurt."

(Now the flower is hitting the microphone.)

"But, if we could excite the atoms of the flower, the effect would be much stronger. Greater power lies in the subtlety of creation."

By this time, the flower has hit the microphone over and over, emphasizing the point.

He continues:

"So, when we get to the subtle phases of these vibrations the power increases, and the power of these vibrations is the power to purify, to increase and to improve the quality of life."

Now he has the flower, a red rose, in one hand. Gentle fingers are dividing the petals until the heart of the flower is exposed.

Again:

"This power of the vibrations is found increasing as we go towards the subtler and subtler fields of creation; thereby, one dive we take into the Absolute, and very powerful influence we create for supplementing the life of all creation."

Somehow the "life of all creation" ends up in the heart of the rose. For those who were not accustomed to having so much depth brought forth in such a simple lecture, the beautiful flowers kept mental fatigue and strain at a minimum. I am convinced that the entire play of flowers was for the edification of the listeners. It became a way for innocent flowers to help the audience along the path, leading to the field of the Absolute. Eyes were seeing what ears were hearing.

The discourse continues:

"What do we mean when we say there is a 'fight' between matter and spirit?"

He is looking at the flower now.

"Take an example. We see a flower. The beauty of the flower is there. When the experiencer is completely lost in the experience of the object,

then the object has as if defeated the very existence of the subject. The subject has lost the glory of its own essential nature by the overshadowing influence of the impression of the object."

Now he pauses. Holding the flower in one hand, he rubs his eye with the flower and cups his hand over it. We are looking at a Yogi with one large brown eye and one red rose. The flower overshadowed one eye!

"The subject has lost the glory of its own essential nature by the overshadowing influence of the impression of the object. Seeing the beauty of the flower, the flower alone is there. The object alone is there, and the existence of the subject is not located. The subject has gone. Only the object remains in consciousness. This is the victory of matter over spirit. This is the defeat of the spirit within."

Such powerful words came gently to the ears.

On the petals of flowers the meaning is not lost in oratory. No emotion is aroused. All energy is channeled to absorbing facts within the boundaries of reason.

Here was a wise Master directing the attention of the conscious mind to the moving, colorful flower, while the subtler states of consciousness grasped the deeper significance of every word.

Pursuing the subject still further:

"Matter has thrown the experiencer in the background, thrown the spirit in the background. Only the matter remains, and the spirit, feeling 'Oh, this flower is so beautiful,' fails to realize that its own blissful, essential nature has been simultaneously annihilated. The experiencer is not found when only the flower remains."

Then the answer to the problem comes:

"What is to be done? The experiencer should enjoy the flower yet not

lose his identity. Then the glory of the flower is enjoyed, and the existence of the experiencer is not lost."

These two points were very important to us. No one sitting in the lecture hall had any desire to be a recluse or renounce the world. Here was a man telling us that we did not have to stay out of all activity of the world; our purpose was to live a life where matter and spirit do not overshadow each other. All life, mental, physical and spiritual, must be lived and yet maintain its status. It must be integrated.

At this moment we were aware of experiencing just that. We were completely aware of ourselves, serene, divine and happy in nature, and aware of the lovely long-stemmed rose.

As he spoke, Maharishi simply and innocently wove the rose between his toes so that the very heart of the flower adorned his foot.

Without moving my head, I glanced slowly about to see smiles playing around the corners of almost everyone's mouth. Only a few men, totally immersed in the thought, had given no notice to the rose.

Knowledge of the Absolute was received as innocently and naturally as air and sunshine. As eye met eye and travelled back to the adorned foot, enjoyment was shared and smiles developed into laughter. Gentle undertones of laughter, which did not break into the feeling, rippled throughout the lecture.

Maharishi, whose philosophy is, "Life is essentially bliss," was pleased to see and hear the happiness. He smiled too, seemingly unaware of the innocent cause of our joy.

By now we were curious to see what would happen to the entwined rose! It sat there happily, unconcerned about its future.

Maharishi picked up another rose and continued:

"If the material glories of life can be further brightened by the light of the inner self, everyone is for it. And here is the technique, the way to accomplish that. Otherwise, if there comes a voice calling 'Oh, you'll be divine and you'll be godly, and you'll become the master of nature, but you must stop looking at flowers, stop enjoying life, refrain from the joys of the senses, get away, just be, live a life in seclusion to become the master of nature,' nobody will hear it."

We were hearing everything! We were absorbing the desire for Being through our senses and our more subtle faculties. He made the Kingdom of Heaven within so real that we could see it, feel it, hear it, and almost taste the bliss he mentioned. And we were glad that to enjoy the bliss we were not required to stop enjoying the roses which were delighting us this evening.

We wondered what would follow next in the life of that red rose.

The lecture kept unfolding and the rose began unwinding.

"The question comes, 'If God is omnipresent, and God is all glory and God is merciful and Father of all, and if He wants us to enjoy eternal bliss which He has made omnipresent, then why do we not experience His glory all the time?'"

By the time the question ended, the rose once again nested its head in Maharishi's brown, graceful hand.

"We need only to bring the Being from its transcendental state and glorify our lives with its presence. This we do through Transcendental Meditation."

The thought of wanting to know more and more of Being occupied my mind, but mainly I wanted to add that red rose to my collection of souvenirs—remembrances of the delightful moments when the soul receives the living waters that make it bloom. I wanted the rose, but I was well aware that others did too!

Once again his words filled the room:

"Mind is thirsty for great happiness, but the happiness experienced in worldly joys is so small, tiny, meager, just insignificant. It doesn't satisfy the search for happiness of the mind; and mind, not finding any ocean of happiness in the outside world, is only tossed about from point to point."

As he said "point to point," each petal had been removed from the rose stem and now lay in a ruby red mound at his feet.

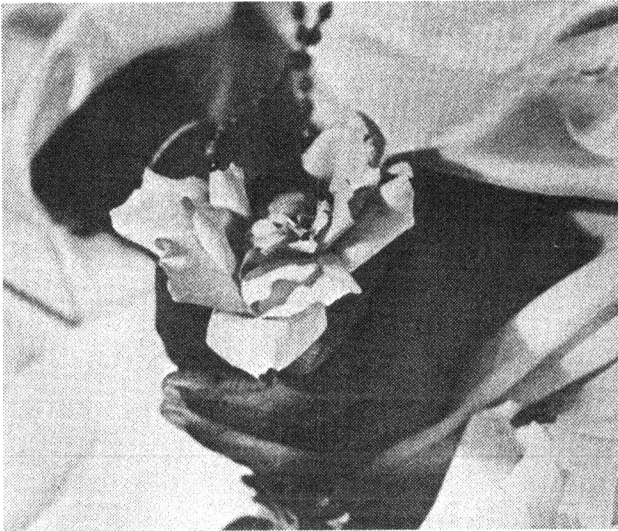

Flowers seem to enjoy being in his hands.

Solomon with all his wisdom, would he have done better? Now there would be petals for all who wished them.

When the lecture was over, joy became unconfined. Everyone crowded around Maharishi. Some wished to present more flowers. Some asked a personal question while others wished to establish a little personal contact. Some were there to invite him to speak at other places for other groups, and still other people extended him invitations to visit interesting sights around the town. To each one who came up he presented a flower. Sitting quietly, I found it pleasant to see all their glowing faces as they walked away with a single flower in their hands.

Below us, as we still lingered in the Transcendental Meditation Center, the noises of the street were making a cacophony of sound. The ebb and flow of the evening traffic, the sharp trill of a siren piercing the night, even the lights from Wilshire Boulevard glowing in our large window failed to disturb the serene enchantment of the evening.

And, in the window of the soul, a little of the curtain had been gently pushed aside to let the light shine in.

Roland and I returned home, and in the privacy of our bedroom discussed the events of the day and evening as was so often our custom before retiring.

"Well," I said, "we've been to lots of lectures and good theater, but I can't think of an evening I ever enjoyed so much as this one. Did you ever see such a delightful sight?"

"Nobody but a Yogi could have played like that with a rose without looking ridiculous," Roland chuckled and added, "I'm not sure just any Yogi could do it, either!"

As I was not tired, I picked up a small paperback copy of William James' book, *The Varieties of Religious Experiences*.

After a time, in his chapter on Conversion, I ran on to a footnote quoting Ralph Waldo Emerson which read:

"When we see a soul

Whose acts are regal, graceful

And pleasant as roses

We must thank God

That such things

Can be

And are."

I put my petals of the rose in an envelope and marked it *Toes and Roses.*

Chapter Ten **The Big Automatic**

Although there were some people who came to Maharishi who might be called extremists, the huge majority were clear thinking men and women who felt his simple technique would relieve them of tensions. For some reason most people were dissatisfied with their religious beliefs and were seeking, just what, they did not seem to know.

"Transcendental Meditation is the non-medicinal tranquilizer," Maharishi would say, *"but that is only one of the by-products. When we plant an apple tree the main purpose is to have apples, but long before the apples are ready, we enjoy the shade of the tree. The shade is a by-product. Release of tension is a by-product of Transcendental Meditation. It is just automatic."*

More and more, Maharishi used the word "automatic" to describe the benefits of the Transcendental Meditation program. Students of yoga, metaphysics and those familiar with the disciplines of religious orders often presented the argument that Maharishi's method sounded too easy. Maharishi would shake his head from side to side, smile and say:

"No need to suffer for the Divine. Our path is the path of bliss. Only a few

minutes you dive morning and evening. You feel fresh and enjoy. Then every-thing is automatic. It is only discontent, lack of bliss that makes man do wrong. When the path to bliss is not known then we must listen to the churches. They point out, 'this is wrong to do,' 'that is right to do,' and we must do that."

"If we practice your technique, Maharishi, will we no longer have need of churches?"

Maharishi would, in his inimitable way, look up and smile at the person asking the question and say,

"What would the world be without churches? You will enjoy churches more because you will understand better what they teach. For those who do not follow churches, Transcendental Meditation will give them an understanding of right and wrong. When one dives within one's self and finds the perfect state of Being, his living and thinking become in-fused with it, and then all good is automatic. You remember the Lord Christ has said, 'Seek ye first the Kingdom of Heaven within, and all else will be added unto thee.'"

As the summer wore on we heard almost the same questions asked over and over and came to realize the needs of people are almost the same.

A question uppermost in the minds of many men was about smoking. One of the first signs to greet the person coming for an interview was the one reading, "No Smoking."

"Oh, no," the harassed person would say as he stamped out his cigarette, "I could never do without smoking."

"Maharishi never asks you to give up anything," the office assis-tants would assure the seeker.

Quite often the answer would be, "If we don't have to give up anything then it can't be any good."

This sort of person would baffle us for a time, but our understanding was growing "automatically" and we began to realize this person would soon be finding fault with everything; he or she was not really going to find the answer in the Transcendental Meditation program or in churches or in science, because the deep desire for real knowledge was not there.

"We do not even think of giving up anything," Maharishi would insist. *"We do whatever our needs demand, but we are regular in practicing Transcendental Meditation, and when we become filled with bliss, with Being, the need is no longer there. There is no need to even think of it. Thinking of something we wish to give up drives the desire for it deeper into the mind, and consequently we desire it more and more."*

To the smoker, he would say, "'When the smoking leaves you, don't try to hold on to it."

Time after time we received reports from those who practiced the Transcendental Meditation technique regularly that they had discontinued smoking without trying and had never been aware of which day or hour they had quit. Generally they just realized that it had been some time since they bought cigarettes. My husband, who smoked sparingly before practicing the Transcendental Meditation technique, was one of the first who realized how completely automatic the change was. There was no suffering, no complaining, no bad effects, no inflicting of experiences, good or bad, on others. One day one simply was aware that smoking was no longer part of life.[10]

But smoking was only a part of the "Big Automatic," as everyone was laughingly calling the Transcendental Meditation program after Maharishi referred to it that way in his lectures. Women who desired to lose weight began to notice as they meditated their need for so much food was lessened. This "automatic" was one of my joys.

Someone asked, "Will we all become renunciates?"

"My technique is for the householder, the man in the world, the man who wants to accomplish more, create more, know more. He can only do more when he is able to go to the source of all power, to Being, to the Absolute, to the field of pure, unbounded awareness. And the journey there is only the first part of it. The second is to bring it back and integrate it into daily life. Then man lives a full life, a life of joy, of peace, of happiness, and a life of great activity, of great creativity. He lives life not one hundred per cent but two hundred per cent! For man, a householder, to go through the world alone is like a wagon rolling along on one wheel. It is better that the two go. The place of woman is important. The woman fills the home with grace, with beauty. She is the balancing point between the positive and the negative.

"Not to have children is like depriving the apple tree of its apples. But no two paths are the same. For those who desire the life of a recluse, for him the life of a recluse is right, and the sound for his meditation is different from the sound given to the householder."

Quite often the question was asked of Maharishi:

"Could you not take any word, any sound, and reduce it to its most subtle state and be able to reach Transcendental Consciousness?" (It is well known that the English poet, Alfred Lord Tennyson, used to repeat his own name over and over before he wrote.)

"Yes," Maharishi answered. *"Any sound can be repeated and repeated until the sound comes to nil; or, you can go the other way and make a sound louder and louder and eventually it also will come to nil. But what we don't know is the effect of the sound on the body, the mind and*

the soul. Each sound has its effect in the universe. Some sounds make people warlike, and some make them peaceful; some make a person retire from activity, and some make more activity. This is the knowledge that has been passed down from our Masters, the Shankaracharya tradition. We know the effects of certain words on certain people. When these words are given and the meditation is regular the effects will be good, all nice, and the man will be happy, content but productive in the world."

"India, then, should be more creative and productive, Maharishi—is this not so?"

"You are right! If this were known in India it would be more creative and better in every way. The fine distinction between the sound unique for a sannyasi or recluse and the sound for a householder has been forgotten, and this loss is established in society. Many have not desired change, but the time is coming when many will listen and India will rise up from her slumbers. It is only necessary that the right sound be used. Already people in India meditate regularly and have great devotion for God."

Maharishi enjoyed lecturing at universities. One engagement at the University of Southern California[11] brought out interesting questions. One in particular made Maharishi laugh, and he quoted it often.

"Why should I take the time to meditate now? I already am happy; I have creative ideas. I will need this more when I am old."

Maharishi said:

"Meditation is not a preparation for death; it is the way to a successful life. Postponing the practice of TM means postponing greater intelligence, greater creativity, greater power and greater happiness. Why not have this when we are young? Why postpone the charm of life to old age?"

Many people, we discovered, came to teachers or sages because they wished to be healed of physical suffering. Many times Maharishi was coaxed to perform a miracle of healing. He would only laugh and shake his head.

"No. If any healing is done, then other greater and greater healings must be done and no one thinks of the practice of meditation. If I start on healing, then I will not have any time left for the Spiritual Regeneration Movement.

"My mission is only to spread the simple technique of Transcendental Meditation; I want to attract good thinking men and women who will be regular in practice. Then, for them, healing will be automatic. Everything pleasing in Nature has healing power. If a child is hurt, healing power is on the lap of mother. A good, pleasing cinema is healing when one is fatigued. Everything charming in Nature has healing power, but Transcendental Meditation has the greatest healing power. It heals the mind, the body, the soul. All life must be healed, not just a part; all must be soothing, harmonious."

Sometimes social workers would bring up the question of the criminal in society. Maharishi said,

"To root out criminal tendencies in the society, it will be necessary to bring satisfaction into the life of the society."

He added:

"People and nations must do as they think right. When the level of the evolution of a people changes, the laws of the society change automatically. If the people in the jails could be taught the Transcendental Meditation program, they could improve themselves automatically." [12]

He continued:

"When they are led to the field of pure Creative Intelligence they no

longer desire to lead a bad life. They will become peaceful and good by nature."

Inevitably, the remark that followed this comment would be, "What effect would the Transcendental Meditation technique have on juvenile delinquency?"[13]

Maharishi's reply:

"Deliquency stems from insecurity, a lack of balance. Transcendental Meditation satisfies that lack. It is best to stop the mischief before it begins. It is natural for children to love. Only direction is needed. Children make mischief when there is not enough love."

Very often in the gatherings were men and women whose lives had been devoted to social betterment. These people questioned Maharishi seriously:

"If the Transcendental Meditation technique can bring about social reform, peaceful relations between nations, and creativity in all fields, would it not be possible to suppose that we could arrive at an ideal state, a 'Utopia'?[14] It might even lead to a Golden Age, comparable to that of Greece and Rome. Would that be possible?"

Maharishi sat soberly.

"Yes, it is possible," he answered.

A question which served to establish Maharishi as a wise man was asked by a child:

"Who made God the Father?"

Maharishi tossed his head gently from side to side, smiled and then said:

"God, the Son, has made God, the Father. No man can be a father until he has a son. The father makes the son, and the son makes the father."

"Why are the people of India starving?" was another common question.

"If the people of India are starving and they are practicing Transcendental Meditation, then it is Karma (a Cosmic Law of Cause and Effect), but it does not mean they are miserable. It is possible to have little to eat and still be happy. In America, where you have so much, people are found to be miserable. It is worse to be miserable in the midst of plenty, of riches, than it is in the midst of poverty."

Another question that came from religious minded people was: "Does not suffering purify?"

"Transcendental Meditation is the greatest purifier," Maharishi would answer, *"and TM is the path to pure happiness. It is the natural tendency of the mind to enjoy more, and it is easy. It is difficult to suffer. A man listening to music will automatically change to a better melody. No one need tell him. He is not satisfied until he hears the best melody. Man is not satisfied with the dew drops, and he need not be. The Almighty Merciful Father has provided an ocean of happiness. Why not take it?*

"And mind does not want long practice or to sit in silence. Mind just will not do it. It is not tempted to the Kingdom of Heaven within because there is no increase of charm. Our technique is not to control the mind. Just satisfy and automatically it goes. We take the easy way.

"We take the easy, the automatic way, and we arrive at the field of pure happiness, and automatically we are happy. We arrive at the source of power, and automatically we are powerful. We arrive at the source of creativity, and we are creative.

"All is ours, and it is ours automatically. Transcendental Meditation is just 'The Big Automatic.'"

Chapter Eleven **Midsummer Night's Schemes**

———————◆●◆———————

Maharishi directed every thought to fulfilling his world mission of spreading the technique of Transcendental Meditation; and the possible approaches to this fulfillment were fascinating and brimming with creative ideas.

He often gathered from ten to twenty of the best minds around him in his room or in the study, and the flow of ideas would start. Newer people immediately suggested calling the President of the United States. Others mentioned names of prominent people who could be contacted. Large magazines were to be approached. Each person gave ideas from his own interest or viewpoint.

Businessmen liked to stress the value of the Transcendental Meditation technique;[15] students stressed scientific approaches, the opening of the deeper levels of consciousness to bring more knowledge into being; women insisted the Transcendental Meditation technique increased grace and the desire for graceful living. They were adamant that its greatest value was of a cosmetic nature: complexions improved, health improved because tensions were released from the body.[16] Faces took on a younger, more pleasing look. But everyone agreed that possibly the greatest gain for the greatest number was that world peace could become a reality.

Maharishi was most pleased with this approach. He answered questions freely and easily. Often he was asked:

"How can a man, by going into silence, affect the peace of the world?"

Maharishi would answer generally in this way:

"The leaders of a nation are not the prime starters of war. They act as the fever or atmosphere of the country demands. If people are full of tension, discontent, the air builds up and action is required. If each man is peaceful within himself he cannot create tensions. And vibrations coming from the deeper levels of consciousness are more powerful—the world could be at peace if only one-tenth of the population of the world meditated." [17]

Then, quite often, the following question would be asked:

"You perhaps call 'peaceful' in India what we in America merely call 'passive.'"

Maharishi's answer:

"No, no, no. In India, meditation is not done properly. Passivity results from too many people using the wrong sound, the wrong medium. One sound is right for a householder and another one for a recluse. Each, used properly, creates the right effect in the atmosphere. Silence is the basic motivating power of activity. Meditation, done properly, will make the householder more active and yet more peaceful, more creative, more loving; and the recluse can achieve what he wants in life."

Questions could go on for hours. Enthusiasm always grew as Maharishi answered each one. Many prominent people were brought to Maharishi and were interested in helping him.

"The East and West are two different worlds," they said. "What is understood by one cannot always be accepted by the other."

Maharishi would smile:

"Transcendental Meditation is not a philosophy or religion. It is a path to Transcendental Consciousness."

Arrangements were made for radio talks, television appearances, and lectures at universities. Many fine people came for personal instruction. Maharishi felt everything moved slowly, but we were constantly amazed at the speed with which the Movement grew.

By midsummer Maharishi announced his plan (or "scheme," as he called a plan), for the First International Convention. It was difficult to think back to the month of May, when Maharishi arrived knowing only two people in Los Angeles! Now, sixteen weeks later, he could talk in terms of a convention!

Arrangements for the convention developed at a rapid rate. For the benefit of those in San Francisco and for those who lived throughout the state of California, Sequoia National Park was chosen. The convention was to be held over a three-day weekend, and plans sounded delightful.

Because of work commitments the Olsons were not able to go, and since Maharishi and his guests were to go to San Francisco for the first part of the week, we seized the opportunity to have our oldest daughter, Melinda, bring her baby daughter from Las Vegas for a visit.

Melinda and baby Kimberly arrived before Maharishi left. Both of my girls adored Maharishi immediately. Melinda learned the Transcendental Meditation technique, and Kimmie could not resist trying to get close enough to Maharishi to play with the

By midsummer (1959) Maharishi announced his plan for The First International Convention at Sequoia National Park, California.

strings of beads he wore about his neck. He kept her entertained by giving her flowers. She and the Siamese cats were constantly being "put out" by the workers and silently invited back by Maharishi.

While Maharishi was a constant delight at all times, his easy, natural way with little children was a joy to behold. The innocent met Innocence on the path and recognition was in the form of happy smiles and the exchange of flowers. Quite often we would see a tiny pair of slippers added to the collection of shoes at Maharishi's door. Then the door would open and a child came out all smiles, eyes bright and shining, arms filled with fruit. Such a sight brought smiles to adult faces and warmth to the heart. It certainly made an unforgettable picture in the mind.

After Maharishi and the others left for Sequoia National Park, we brought in help and gave the house a thorough cleaning.

The absence of our Yogi left an aching void. We couldn't believe how we missed everyone. However, it was a nice time to indulge in simple pleasures like having coffee downstairs in our robes in the morning and washing our clothes at any time it suited our fancies.

Before Melinda left for home, I thought I would "sound her out."

"I've been thinking, I was very impulsive about learning the Transcendental Meditation technique. Maybe I'll give it up for a time...."

Melinda was shocked.

"Please don't do that, Mother. You have no idea what a change I see in you and Daddy. You are so relaxed and happy, so much more patient, gentle and understanding."

Melinda, my oldest child, had always been very dear and close to me. She knew she could be frank in telling me of my improvements, but I was a little shocked as well as amused to hear of my many imperfections—now becoming improved.

We both have a good sense of humor—I couldn't resist saying, "I'm glad the Transcendental Meditation technique has made so many changes in me. Your beautiful Mother's Day cards and gifts led me to believe I was a paragon of perfection." We both laughed.

Thinking of my other daughter and her husband I said, "I do wish you could get Mary and Peter to come over. If they would spend a day with Maharishi I know they would really like him, and perhaps they wouldn't think I am slightly out of my mind."

Melinda laughed. She had just spent a day with her sister and brother-in-law. It seems they had called our home many times during the summer but had gotten tired of hearing strange voices and people who sometimes said, "There's no one here by that name," when they asked for Mr. or Mrs. Olson. They did think I was a little mad. I had called them and tried to interest them in the Transcendental Meditation program on the basis of its being scientific.

"I'll have to see it to believe it. It sounds emotional to me," Peter said with collegiate authority.

"At this very moment, Peter, the house looks like a laboratory; tests are going on in the basement, heart tests have been made, changes in blood chemistry discussed, and other things I don't know about."

They promised to come when summer school was over. Time passed and on Sunday evening, Theresa and I were never away from the front windows, watching for our other family to return.

Finally, cars of laughing, bedraggled people came driving up. The guests had been divided among four cars. Mata-ji looked a bit fatigued, and it was my pleasure to place a tray of ice cold fruit juice in her room.

Maharishi never showed signs of fatigue. The drivers, however, took off again quite hurriedly before schemes for the regeneration of the world could get a foothold in the study. As everyone left, Maharishi actually had the disappointed look of a little child who wanted to play longer, but all his playmates had to take a nap!

Roland and I were anxious to hear about the First Convention, so we sat with him in the study. Between sips of cool apple juice, he told us of the joy he experienced in bringing so many of his family together.

"I shall have a Center in London, too," he stated.

London seemed such a long way off. How would this little man find anyone to listen to him in London? But, then, how was it that he had found anyone here in Los Angeles!

"The best part of it all," continued Maharishi, "was that we decided on a Three Year Plan. Since the technique of Transcendental Meditation must be handed down person to person, it will take a long time for me to spread my message. But I can train some people very carefully; then they, too, can do it; and I can train hundreds of Guides who can teach and check experiences. If we have Spiritual Guides instructing in all parts of the world, and Meditation Guides teaching the value of Transcendental Meditation, it will all go very fast, and the world can soon be entirely at peace."

The magnitude of this plan stunned me. It seemed reasonable

that even as powerful a personality as Maharishi could use more help.

Roland was quite interested.

"How will you put this in operation?"

"The best way is to establish a headquarters and then invite people to come to a training course for three months," said Maharishi.

"Possibly in India?" asked Roland. "Or why not Los Angeles?"

Charlie Lutes, who had just returned for some papers, answered that question. "Can you imagine the shock if someone asks us where we received our training to teach the Transcendental Meditation technique and we said, "Seventh and Broadway in Los Angeles!"

Maharishi laughed. "India would be best," he said.

We had been hearing from Lachsman, Mata-ji's brother, how inexpensive it was to build and how little food costs in India by comparison with Los Angeles.

Plans, or schemes, for the International Meditation Academy began to gather momentum like a snowball rolling downhill. Every day when we came home they were bigger and bigger. An artist in the group made a drawing; an architect drew a set of plans; the site was to be in a high valley close to the Himalayas in Uttar Kashi.

"Here," said Maharishi, "the air is pure; no one has lived here except wandering sannyasi who meditate constantly. The source of the Ganges is close and the crystal clear stream flowing through this valley becomes India's famous river. No smoking, no alcohol, no violence have ever been known there."

We were like children listening to the "Promised Land." The

"schemes" of the Spiritual Regeneration Movement were mild in comparison to the schemes the meditators had for getting to the Meditation Academy in India, the Academy which, at that point, had not even been started.

Maharishi, accompanied by founding members of S.R.M., goes for a walk.

I had hundreds of impractical ideas. Roland had one practical answer to each of them. "No!"

"Maharishi, I want to go to India and live in that beautiful valley. Can't I?" I pleaded.

Maharishi was quiet for a few seconds. Then he smiled a little.

"You will come when it is suitable for ladies." His eyes twinkled. "When you can have your electric blanket. It is very cold at night. But you will go there." (It was Roland's and my great delight to spend three months at the academy in Rishikesh in 1966.)

"What will you do?" we would ask him.

"What is there to do? I just go. It all comes out."

"But, Maharishi," the ladies would say with eyes brimming, "you'll be so alone."

"I never feel alone."

One who often sat with Maharishi was Lois Hague. Lois looked about twenty, but from her mature comments we realized she must be older. In talking with her I discovered an interesting background. She was an only child brought up in a carefully supervised religious atmosphere in the Midwest. She had always had strong religious tendencies and, in her teens, joined a group that went about the countryside preaching and singing evangelical songs.

"Somehow," said Lois, "I still felt the need for something more."

Lois and our family knew the New Testament quite well. We both quoted from it often and were surprised at how much clearer the meanings and the beliefs of Christ were becoming to us.

Although Maharishi said he had not read the New Testament, he seemed to say many of the same things quoted in it. He constantly referred to the Kingdom of Heaven within, the great Lord Christ and so on.

So many questions after the lectures concerned the divinity of Christ; did He exist at all; the possibility that only Christ consciousness exists.

To each, Maharishi, sometimes shocked, would reply that

there is no doubt as to the existence of the great Lord Christ; He unquestionably was a Divine Incarnation; one could not possibly separate the person from his state of consciousness. The great Lord Christ had brought the world salvation, but, "His message is not understood."

Maharishi then announced to the group that he would like to bring out a booklet containing the ideas that had come up during the Convention in Sequoia. He laid out plans in terms of three years. There were to be three Three Year Plans.

One typewriter was not enough to take care of all the new creative activity. The dining room table groaned under added weight. Women who worked all day rushed over as quickly as possible, presented Maharishi with flowers, and typed half the night.

The writing and re-writing of the First Three Year Plan was fascinating. A sentence would be thrown out in the air. Five or six people made suggestions or corrections until the original thought seemed gone forever. Those who had any experience in writing stood it bravely. Then Maharishi would suggest, "Shall we say...," and the idea again took form.

Somehow I began to get the idea that we were receiving some sort of training. Dr. Hislop showed the most flexibility since the writing was his responsibility. He would write an excellent passage. While it was being read, strangers would enter the study. Maharishi would say to them:

"What you think?"

We would brace ourselves as they suggested ideas carefully thought out but unrelated to the topic.

Maharishi would beam at them and say to Dr. Hislop, "Put that in." The color would rise in Dr. Hislop's already florid complexion, but, in a quiet, controlled voice he would say simply, "Just as you wish, Maharishi."

Although Dr. Hislop knew very well he would be criticized if

Maharishi with Mata-ji, Helen and Charlie Lutes. Helen and Charlie were with Maharishi daily and accompanied him on all his trips.

the writing didn't make sense, he never made an audible comment. The discipline in the leaders of our group was most impressive.

Equally impressive was the Vice-President, Charles Lutes.

"Charlie," as Maharishi called him affectionately, was on hand every evening to drive Maharishi to the lecture or wherever he wished to go. A tall, handsome man, Charlie was top salesman for a large cement company. Most of the comments Charlie made were sensible and rather erudite.

Maharishi was always drawn to the clear-thinking, practical person, and it was easy to see a great affection build up for Charlie.

It was Charlie who finally saved the day for the Three Year Plan. After a long session of new comments and endless *bon mots*, Charlie gathered all the papers from the typists, took Dr. Hislop by the arm, and said firmly, "I'm taking all this to the printer."

Maharishi only smiled.

Somehow the two men brought order out of it all, and a reasonably presentable booklet was proferred.[18]

While the number of Guides and the number of Meditation Centers mentioned in the booklet were overly ambitious, the basic plans laid down were completely carried out before the three years elapsed.

Chapter Twelve **Jai Guru Dev**

In the latter part of August, a good number of meditators couldn't be pried away from '433' except for dire necessities, like making a living. More than one homemaker was heard to say, "My house is a sight, but I don't care. I want to spend every possible minute with Maharishi."

We felt the same way, but we seemed to see him less and less. Many were content to come and sit in the living room all day or in the garden and see him for just a few seconds as he went to a lecture. Since all my work was finished at the theater and I only had to put in an occasional brief appearance, I had more time at home but seemed to spend it with Mata-ji.

A glorious Sunday in the last week of August was an exception. After a summer of cooking, washing, and ironing most of the women were glad to have a little rest. Sheela had long ago given over to Mata-ji, and Mata-ji used to say, as she handed a large basket of ironing to anyone who came through the kitchen:

"Blessings?"

In India it is considered a great blessing to serve a Master. Most of the women were not so concerned over the blessings as the personal joy of doing something for Maharishi. But if one of the sight-seeing trips developed, ironing, cooking, and washing were dropped and everyone scurried to be on hand at the door. Maharishi never disappointed them. It was a joy to hear him say, "Come, come," and to see everyone scramble into cars and be off like happy, unworried children.

As there had been a trip on Saturday, the kitchen was a sight on Sunday. Helen Lutes, Christina Granville and others phoned to offer help. I refused, glad for everyone to get a little rest and delighted to have the house and Maharishi to myself. Mata-ji and her brother were so popular that they were invited to two or three affairs a day; Ram Rao had been called back to India on business. Because it was Sunday, most of the group were taking care of home duties.

It didn't take too long to establish order and start Maharishi's dinner. It was the first time I had cooked for him, and I wanted very much to please him. I simply could not stop cooking. I had something in every pot in the house—all vegetables. At least he would have quantity if not quality. I hoped for both.

Remembering a special almond cookie I thought he might like, I started mixing them and then couldn't resist a fruit salad because of the tempting, luscious fruits the students brought. Turning away from the sink, I found Maharishi sitting at the kitchen table, his big brown eyes shining with laughter and his face looking like a little boy's, saying:

"I'm hungry."

"Oh, Maharishi, I'll bring your dinner right away. I didn't realize it was so late."

Because he did not eat breakfast, dinner was usually served him in the study between twelve and one o'clock. It was now one-thirty.

He laughed and said casually, "I'll stay here."

I was glad Mata-ji was not there. She would not have allowed such informality, but for us it was delightful.

While Maharishi was eating, I asked him about Mata-ji.

"Mata-ji has married into one of the oldest, wealthiest families in Calcutta. They live according to the old traditions. All the families live together in a large apartment building, and the elders rule. They are very strict. Mata-ji is not allowed to go on the street without her face covered. It is unusual that she could come here."

It was quite a big jump from the shelter of such a life to the freedom of Hollywood. Mata-ji was to be admired for the balanced way she had accepted life here. No wonder she was so often puzzled!

"Maharishi, Ram Rao told us Mata-ji is considered to be a saint in India. How do you define sainthood?"

"A saint is said to do no harm in the world."

By now a few people had come in and were sitting around the kitchen and we discussed the answer. It satisfied me, although I was used to thinking of saints in relation to miraculous deeds. A person who did no physical, mental or spiritual harm in the world would have to be godly. It was hardly a human possibility. Certainly Mata-ji was active in the world, and we could see no harm in her. Maharishi insisted quite often that spirituality must meet the test of activity in the world to prove itself.

After lunch Maharishi retired to his room, and I tackled the mountain of ironing. The silk was lovely to touch, and as the neatly folded mounds of silk garments grew, I felt a great satisfaction in place of fatigue. Having grown up with an example of a "fussy" ironer in our dear little "Grammie," Roland's mother, I felt confident they would please Mata-ji.

I had not quite finished when Mata-ji and a large group of women who had taken her to lunch came home.

When Mata-ji discovered me ironing and glanced over the finished work, she was both pleased and upset.

"Must rest," she said to me like a little mother.

Someone else took the ironing. Mata-ji beckoned to me. "Come, come," she sounded like Maharishi.

I followed her upstairs to her little room. On her bed were spread dozens of saris, exquisite creations of beautifully intricate designs, artistic color and elegant silk.

She motioned for me to take one.

"Oh, Mata-ji, I couldn't!"

Mata-ji could be very imperious.

"You take," she commanded firmly.

We had heard from Ram Rao that saris were valued anywhere from $50 to $400. After looking them all over, I picked one with a small design on it and a green border. She brought out a lovely embroidered cotton petticoat that went from one's waist to the floor. A string went through the waistband. Everything depended on this string. It was pulled very tightly and tied, and the sari was tucked in it.

She demonstrated it and showed me how hers was put on. It looked quite simple. I went to my room to try it on. In a few moments squeals of laughter meant others were receiving saris also.

The sari wasn't so simple to put on after all. Five yards is a lot of silk, and somewhere a few yards spilled out no matter what I did.

The laughter upstairs brought Maharishi out of his room. Two or three women who could manage the saris and looked beautiful in them, invited him into the garden for picture taking. He was delighted with their appearance and commented:

"Ah, nice. Very graceful."

A few women joined me in my bedroom while we tried to figure out ways and means of pinning it on me. Pins are never used by the women in India, and we, too, felt it would be a pity to put pins through such lovely silk. Emily, who was handy at everything, could keep hers on, so she was trying to help all the rest of us who were having difficulty. There was much comment on the beautiful line they gave women.

"Isn't it a pity women here don't wear these lovely things instead of going around in shorts and capris?"

"I wonder how they would be for working around the house and taking care of the children," one of the younger women said.

"Mata-ji manages so easily and always makes a graceful picture. I think a sari has more appeal than shorts and slacks. When you think of it, our clothes are not too comfortable. I think I'll dress like this all the time." This was my remark, but, of course, I was not serious about doing it. However, I would have liked the idea—if I could ever get it on—to stay.

Just then someone called up the stairs.

"Someone asking for you, Mrs. Olson."

I thought it was one of the new meditators who had left something here, as they did so often, so I sailed down the stairs with hands full of the new sari that I couldn't keep tucked in—and promptly met my daughter Mary and her husband, Peter. I gasped at the sight of them—in shorts. Extra short it seemed to me.

Mary gave me a quick hug, picked up one end of the sari and said, "What in the world have you got on?"

I was wishing I could drape some of it on her.

Before I could answer, a pack of giggling women led by Emily came down the stairs. We were still in the front hall. Emily, who had beautiful long hair, had let it down, Indian style, and pinned a red hibiscus over one ear. She was carrying more of the flowers and gave me one on the way to the garden.

I heard someone say, "Who is THAT?"

Emily answered, "Mrs. Olson's family."

Peter took the hibiscus. His black eyes twinkled. "Here, let me pin it on you. Are those the scientists you've been telling me about?"

"Never mind. Let's go in the dining room and visit."

I thought we could close the door and have some privacy. I looked my children over supposedly from an "outsider's" point of view. A more handsome couple didn't exist. Peter was well built, over six feet tall with dark, curly hair. Mary was a lovely looking girl. She carried her father's blond Scandinavian features and had much poise and serenity of her own.

If only they were dressed differently!

"We just came by to say a quick hello to you and Daddy," said Mary. "We have a tennis date, and I must have left my racquet in the garage."

At this point nothing would have meant more to me than for

Mary and Peter to have met a solid, serious looking group of people and to have presented my precious daughter and her likable husband to Maharishi in clothes more suitable for the eyes of a Yogi from the Himalayas.

"You stay here. I'll call Daddy. I'm sure he knows where your racquet is."

Roland usually spent Sunday making little repairs and seeing to things in general around the house. I could hear him in the basement now. Since this had been converted into a scientific laboratory to determine the increase in the amount of light on the face during meditation, he was trying to make the cellar more comfortable.

"No, no, don't bother Daddy. We'll meet him for lunch as soon as summer school is over. I think I know where my racquet is."

And they headed for the garden.

Women in saris, wearing hibiscus in their hair, were floating everywhere. Maharishi, Mata-ji and Lachsman were having a picture taken with a few of them.

If there was ever a time when East and West did not meet, this was it! An understandable gasp went through the garden as the two barelegged youngsters joined the group. I was sure Mata-ji had never seen a man—or a woman for that matter—in shorts, and I hoped she wouldn't faint!

"My daughter and son-in-law are going to play tennis, and they have come for a racquet," I explained to Maharishi.

"Perfectly natural," he said and went on about the business of taking pictures.

It was easy to read Peter's mind. He always thought I was a little off-beat. Because of his fine mind and good sense of humor, somehow I hoped he would join the group, but now I knew it was a lost cause. The whole situation was too incongruous!

Maharishi and meditators in the garden. From left to right: Ram Rao, Lachsman, Ron Sheridan, Maharishi, Helen Lutes, Charlie Lutes, Mata-ji, Helena Olson, Roland Olson, Emily Lee.

Looking about the garden, Peter noticed a wire coming from Maharishi's bedroom window to the Meditation House. In reply to his questioning glance, I simply said, "Oh, that…." I really didn't want to discuss it. It was a communication system thought up by one of the engineers. It enabled Maharishi to spend more time in his bedroom since he could press a button and talk to new meditators in the meditation booths and they could answer. It was serviceable and a source of much pleasure to Maharishi. But I felt

188

Peter would not be impressed. Also, I wasn't interested in having either of them stay around the garden dressed as they were!

"Come on Peter, we're late now." Mary sensed my embarrassment and tried to help.

As we went back into the house, somehow the screen door banged shut and caught my sari in it. It was snatched off me entirely.

We all had to laugh. Thank goodness for the cotton petticoat! There is nothing like a good laugh to relieve a tense situation.

Mary gathered up the sari and fell in love with the beautiful silk. She probably would have tried putting it on if Peter hadn't rushed her out.

Watching them drive away, I was filled with mixed emotions. The Transcendental Meditation program had come to mean so much to me. In such a short time it had provided me with a sense of inner security, a balance. It had strengthened my purpose and, at the same time, I was still able to take life lightly. My health, which had always been delicate, was improving every day even though the strains on it increased. I wanted my children to share all these joys, but I knew this was a personal matter. It was not something to be forced or pushed. It can only be offered. We had offered it, but their time did not seem to be right for accepting.

In the last few evenings that Maharishi was with us, the midsummer scheming gave way to serious plans for New York—Maharishi's next stop.

Ron Sheridan was to go ahead and select a hotel room. Arrangements had to be made for lectures, for more publicity and for more organization. The mission of spreading spiritual regeneration had to go on. Everyone begged Maharishi to stay in Los Angeles forever and let the world come to him.

Roland made quite substantial arguments in favor of this, and Maharishi looked at him with amusement and love as Roland recited the practical reasons for Maharishi staying in Los Angeles.

"I must go, but I will come back again," Maharishi said softly. The promise of having more delightful times with our dearly loved Yogi made the thought of parting a little more bearable.

Thirty to forty people were in the house all the time, yet their presence added to our joy. The sharing of so many delights developed a strong bond of love and friendship. All of us were anxious to bask in the warmth of Maharishi's presence. Each tried to show appreciation and affection by aiding him in his one heart's desire— his world mission.

Time, ideas, love, and money were offered. The money raised from personal instruction was for the Movement, not to benefit Maharishi but rather the people who would be able to come into his presence, hear his simple message, practice the Transcendental Meditation technique and go on their way. It was impossible to give him anything for himself. Although gifts poured in, he accepted the thought only and passed on the articles.

"What shall we give Maharishi for a farewell gift?" was asked all day long.

Discussing it with Mata-ji through an interpreter, we discovered something that could be done.

"Maharishi would like a Puja."

"Puja" didn't mean anything to me and so we went to Lois. Lois knew about Pujas and took over the arrangements. We learned a

Puja was a ceremony held in thanksgiving for some happy occasion. In India it is both a religious ceremony and a festival. In this Puja a traditional homage is made to Guru Dev and to the bestowers of pure knowledge throughout the ages. Fruit and flowers are offered, small candles made from sweet butter and cotton are lit, and each individual offers prayers to God.

Great preparations had to be made in the hall. It was expected that over a hundred people would attend. Not all the meditators were to be notified as many lived some distance away.

The chairs were moved close to the wall and long, low tables were set up and covered with white cloths (sheets, to be truthful!). Candles, incense, and pictures of Maharishi's beloved Master were placed everywhere, and plates of cookies and baskets of fruits and nuts gave a festive, colorful and fragrant atmosphere.

We started dressing early for the Puja. All the ladies who had saris planned to wear them. Almost everyone sailed about quite gracefully and naturally in them except me. I still had a bad time keeping mine on!

Maharishi and his entourage from '433' arrived at the hall a little early. Each person was given a small paper plate with flower petals and the small candle. From where I sat on the floor near the dais, it was exciting to see the sumptuous tables, the eyes of men and women glowing like live coals in the candlelight, and to smell the fragrance of pungent incense and the delicate scent of roses throughout the room. The beautiful saris made large splashes of color as the ladies moved about.

The ceremony started with silence, each individual meditating along with the Master.

"When two or three are gathered in My Name," went through my mind and I truly felt the presence of God. It was easy to understand that each person felt the same because it was the union of all in meditation that brought it about.

Quietly, Maharishi started chanting. We followed the examples of Mata-ji and Lois, who threw a few petals at the pronouncement of each name.

During the last part, all the candles on the plates were lit. Hindu chants were given by Mata-ji and her brother, Lachsman.

At the Puja, sitting on the floor near the dais...Christine Granville, Helen Lutes, Jessamine Verrill, David Verrill, Emily Lee.

Maharishi asked for prayers to be said and nodded in our direction. Roland and I started the "Our Father." Everyone joined in. It was like the roar of the ocean and gave a deep feeling of satisfaction to all who had been trained in the Christian tradition.

Afterwards prayers of all types were said. Many men surprised us with simple, beautiful prayers. Some were established church prayers, some were from the heart and memories of childhood. The air was filled with love and devotion. God became reality, and it was natural to open our hearts and express our sincerest and deepest thoughts.

Lois sang a beautiful, simple song dating back to her evangelical days. The "Ave Maria" was sung and said in Latin, Spanish, German and Portuguese. Affirmations came from those who followed Religious Science.

A long silence indicated the prayers were over.

Then it was time for the party.

All helped themselves to the refreshments. Mata-ji had brought many gold medals with enameled pictures of Guru Dev on them. She asked Theresa to pass these out to anyone who wanted one.

Then, from a bracelet on her arm, she took an unusually beautiful medal of Guru Dev seated on a gold lotus and presented it to me. Maharishi told me later that the Maharanee of the province where Mata-ji lived had presented it to her and it was precious to her. Blessed Mata-ji! She proved the true value of the Transcendental Meditation program to me every day, and her treasured gift has served to enshrine her in my heart.

The party lasted quite some time. Slides taken by the meditators were shown as well as a few movies. Maharishi laughed at the sight of himself on the screen and once in a while would say, "Show it again," if the picture happened to be quite good.

Everyone was happy, and morning seemed a long way off. However, the Puja had to come to an end and it was inevitable that it should come…the dawn of the last day of Maharishi's visit.

Since he wanted to stop in San Francisco once again before he left for New York, Maharishi accepted the offer of one of the group to drive him north. The plans were that they should leave at eight o'clock in the morning.

Everyone was up and about early. People stayed discreetly on the front lawn as packing was going on all over the house. Mata-ji had been presented many gifts, and her big cases were filled to overflowing. She intended giving these gifts to people in India.

"Mata-ji, please don't give this away," I said as I gave her five yards of delicate nylon with sprays of embossed white flowers. "Please use this for a sari. You don't have to iron it." Mata-ji was amazed and pleased and promised to keep it.

Lachsman had to carry his excess baggage in cartons. No one realized that he had been buying tape recorders, polaroid cameras, and other things that he could not find in India. He also had evidence of the generosity of his new American friends.

Maharishi's new case was filled to capacity, and he needed a separate box for tapes of the lectures to be played in other cities. There were also printed pamphlets to help save him time in New York.

With all of this to move, the gentleman who was to chauffeur Maharishi arrived in a Volkswagen! He must have pictured in his mind taking only Maharishi and his little carpet roll. Fortunately, he also owned an Opel station wagon and promptly went home to get it. As he packed this he had to get more air in the tires! The car, however, still sat lower and lower in the street!

People with arms full of flowers lined the walks. A few remembered to bring cameras. The moment before he was to get in the car,

Maharishi invited Roland, Theresa and me to have a picture with him. After rushing around all morning none of us felt quite prepared for a picture; but Maharishi motioned to Lou Lee, and Lou set about taking it with color film, although the morning was quite overcast and he doubted it would print well. It not only came out but is quite unusual, a proper remembrance of a wonderful summer.

Maharishi with Roland, Helena and daughter Theresa. "An unusual remembrance of a wonderful summer."

One by one, each meditator came to the car window to receive a flower and a blessing. This rare person, this charming yet serene personality, had touched our lives with his natural, loving ways, and now we had to part with him. Faces were composed, but all eyes brimmed with tears that could not spill over. It was good to have the flowers to wave, to give the hands something to do, and to bury one's face in!

Maharishi, accompanied by Mata-ji and Lachsman, leaves '433'.

Waiting my turn to go up to the car window, I knew I could not say anything. There was too much to be thankful for: his presence in our home; the laughter in the rooms; the puzzled looks on his face as he tried to understand us; the comedies and anxieties he shared with us; the chants in the bath; the play with the children and the Siamese cats; the beautiful, flower-filled days; the big, happy family that assembled about him. All this he had brought us, and even more important, the sacred, quiet peace of the soul.

No, it was not possible to speak. Just present one's flower and smile.

The throng pushed closer to the car as it slowly started down Harvard Boulevard, away from '433'.

After a good laugh over the possibility that the packed little car might not be able to make it, we waved our flowers and whispered the benediction our beloved Master had taught us:

"Jai Guru Dev…Maharishi…"

JAI GURU DEV

Postscript **by Helena Olson**

—————◆◆◆—————

Gratitude to the Smiths

"Curly" (Gerald A.), Georgette, and Christy.
In the aura of their friendship, and in the hospitality of
their home, I found the right atmosphere for writing
more about Maharishi at '433'.

Now it is 1975, and Maharishi has declared this time to be the dawn of the Age of Enlightenment.

"It is still dark," he said, in January of 1975 in Hertenstein, Switzerland, to thousands of his leaders, teachers, international staff, and international press, "but, dawn comes out of darkness; and the few streaks of light tell us more Light is coming. Through the window of science we see the dawn of the Age of Enlightenment."

For me, although there was no formal declaration, 1959 was "The Coming of the Light of Intelligence." In a time when the experience of people was war, economic instability, breakdown of authority of church, state, school and family, there was a faint ray of hope brought by a Yogi from Uttar Kashi, Himalayas, India, who announced with simplicity to his first Western audience:

"I have come to say to all the world that man was not born to suffer; he was born to enjoy."

He explained this state happened naturally through a simple, mental technique which he was prepared to give to everyone in the world. As I sat with him in 1972 in Mallorca, Spain, in a small hotel room, I could not help but be awed by the magnitude of the ideas as he announced an admittedly ambitious World Plan to solve the age-old problems of mankind in this generation: a trained, qualified teacher for each 1,000 people around the globe, a World Plan Center for every million population, the work to be accomplished in four years.

1972   was the Year of Knowledge.
       (Developing and perfecting publicity materials, pamphlets,
       expositions, and planning Teacher Training Courses.)

1973   was the Year of Activity.
       (Conducting international symposia attended by
outstanding scientists and lecturers on art, science, literature,
as well as by Nobel Laureates. Personal visits by Maharishi
       to many countries. Holding Teacher Training Courses in
       various countries.)

1974 was the Year of Achievement.
(Appointing qualified teachers of Transcendental
Meditation to countries throughout the world. Holding
Teacher Training Courses. Solidifying Maharishi
International University. Courses on the Science of Creative
Intelligence® becoming part of international educational
systems.)

1975 was the Year of Fulfillment; the Dawn of the Age of
Enlightenment. (Strengthening all avenues of communication—writing, television and radio. Founding Maharishi
European Research University whose major goals were to
perform research on higher states of consciousness and to
develop practical procedures for developing these higher states.)

Only the names of the years were laid out by Maharishi in 1972. I
could not help saying to him, "But Maharishi, from the first day
you came out of the Himalayas you have had a World Plan."
Maharishi smiled gently. "Yes, it is so," he said, "only now, a World
Plan has become THE WORLD PLAN."

It was Maharishi's way of expressing his vast ideas in such simple
and charming expressions that made the handful of people who
gathered around him in Los Angeles during the summer of 1959
confident of being able to carry out his every wish in order to bring
this practical knowledge of living the fullness of life to everyone.

Generally, I loved to agree with all the grandeur in the air, but
secretly I had a few doubts. There's just a little handicap, I thought.
He doesn't know the world. He knows only a few people in India, a
few in California. He has no obvious means of support, no press

agent, no advance man, no booking agent, no publicity material. He is one man, a monk with no possessions, but with an idea that all people in the world could be made happy. How beautiful! Doubts were put aside, speculating put aside, activity welcomed, and accomplishments came quickly.

Throughout the entire summer of 1959 Maharishi had asked, almost implored, to speak with scientists. We attributed this to his own scientific background (he had studied physics at Allahabad University). A few times people came for the technique and put on the first questionnaire "scientist" where occupation was requested. This caused a ripple of excitement; but generally these people, very sincere in what they called science, were not the caliber for which Maharishi was looking. Even so, he spent hours discussing experiments with whosoever came, trying to awaken deeper interest in exploring the effects of the Transcendental Meditation technique on the body. When one man was sure he could record light on the face while the person meditated, Maharishi called Roland into the study. "Where could we make a scientific laboratory in the house?" The house, since Maharishi had entered it, bulged in all its fourteen rooms. Occasionally even our bedroom and dressing room were invaded when we were not home.

"How about the basement?" suggested Roland.

"Too dark," said one man. Maharishi smiled and said, "Just right for the study of light."

So Roland set about fixing up the basement. All that was needed was to find a new place for Christmas tree ornaments, outgrown baby furniture, gift boxes too good to throw away, and all the paraphernalia that a housewife saves. I am not sure where Roland put most of it, but I have seen very little of it since; and an un-cluttered laboratory emerged. Many tests were carried out in the improvised laboratory. Generally, Maharishi would shake his head from side to side and say, "It is too crude. We need finer instruments." But none appeared. Those of us who were experiencing the first joys and benefits of the Transcendental Meditation program were puzzled by Maharishi's interest in science. Who could guess in 1959 that a message brought to the world by a Yogi from the Himalayas would one day be classified as scientific; and therefore, the benefits and effects would be scientifically repeatable and easily proven through scientific investigation. Yet only through such a procedure would masses eventually adopt Transcendental Meditation leading to 1975 being called the Year of Fulfillment. We had taken it to our hearts, but mental understanding and proof is more substantial.

My one and only attempt to satisfy Maharishi's plea for scientists was not successful. One hot August day, I called the Science Department at UCLA. I was passed from one department head to another because I would not give up. Citing the benefits to health, I was shuttled to the Medical Department. I explained at great length how this meditation immediately brought changes into the bodily functions and gave improvement and relief to illnesses.[19] Because it had amazed me, I quoted as an example, a young epileptic.

"Although she has a serious form of epilepsy, since she began meditating she has had fewer and fewer seizures." All to no avail.

So it followed, naturally, that a meditating graduate student at UCLA chose for his thesis, "The Physiological Effects of

Transcendental Meditation." Dr. Robert Keith Wallace presented a paper of such clarity, fully substantiated with tests on fine instruments, that *Science*, a leading scientific magazine, published it in 1972; and Maharishi's interest in science was immediately justified. A stir was created in the scientific world, and hundreds of scientists began exacting tests and thereby expanded the knowledge and benefits of Transcendental Meditation.[20] Over it all presides a Yogi with an appreciation for authentic verification who smilingly gives his blessing to the findings of the scientists; and this has given rise to the Scientific Charts. See Appendices B and C for descriptions and examples of scientific charts that verify the benefits of the Transcendental Meditation technique discussed in this book.

Appendix A A Brief Introduction to the Maharishi Vedic Technologies

• • •

Just what is the Transcendental Meditation technique? How does it work? What are the advanced Vedic technologies that are mentioned in various places in the book? Here you will find brief explanations of these various techniques that Maharishi has brought out to fully develop each individual's spiritual potential to the highest state of human development—enlightenment.

The *Transcendental Meditation* Technique

The Transcendental Meditation technique of His Holiness Maharishi Mahesh Yogi is a simple, natural, effortless procedure that is practiced for 15–20 minutes twice daily while sitting comfortably with eyes closed. This Vedic technique is easy to learn and does not require any special beliefs, behavior or lifestyle changes. Adults and children of all cultures, religions and educational backgrounds can learn the technique and use it to full advantage.

The Transcendental Meditation technique systematically takes the attention from the conscious thinking level to more subtle and abstract levels of thinking until we transcend the subtlest thought activity and experience pure consciousness, the simplest state of human awareness, unmixed with thought activity.

Pure consciousness is a state of infinite silence. Maharishi calls this state Transcendental Consciousness, a field of Being.

In this state the individual mind is quiet yet awake to its own essential nature. It knows itself. Because it knows itself and nothing else, we call it a state of self-referral consciousness.

During our 15-20 minute session of meditation, we can experience Transcendental Consciousness many times. As the activity of the mind settles down, the body gains deep rest and releases accumulated stress, thereby revitalizing the entire nervous system. When we come out of meditation, we find we are more creative, more refreshed, and that life goes a bit better. Those who practice the Transcendental Meditation technique regularly find improvements in mental activity, physiological health, and social interactions both at home and at the office. The scientific charts included in Appendix C give us a glimpse of these confirmed findings.

The *TM-Sidhi* Program

An advanced Vedic technology is the TM-Sidhi program. According to Maharishi, with regular practice of this Vedic technology, the conscious mind learns to think and act from the simplest state of human awareness, the silent field of Being—Transcendental Consciousness. This ability enables us to actualize the dynamic creative potentiality of this field for greater effectiveness and success in daily life.

During the TM-Sidhi program the mind entertains certain

phrases called *Sutras*. If we think these *Sutras* from the ordinary surface level of thinking, with which we are all familiar, they have no noticeable effect. But when these *Sutras* are introduced at the level of Being, Transcendental Consciousness, they actually stir infinite silence into specific channels of manifestation. The silence is made dynamic.

Practicing the TM-Sidhi program results in increased coordination between mind and body and greater support of Nature in fulfilling our hopes and desires for a better life.

Yogic Flying

One of the *Sutras* practiced during the TM-Sidhi program is Yogic Flying. Yogic Flying demonstrates perfect mind-body coordination and is correlated with maximum brain-wave coherence.

The action of flying actually originates from Transcendental Consciousness. During Yogic Flying, the body responds to the mind's intention, on the level of Transcendental Consciousness, by spontaneously lifting off the ground and moving in a particular direction. There are three stages of Yogic Flying: lifting off and moving in a series of short hops; lifting off and hovering in the air, and lifting off and flying through the air.

Even from the first stage of Yogic Flying, when the body lifts up in a series of short hops, the Yogic Flyer inwardly experiences bubbling bliss and exhilaration while automatically generating an outer influence of increased coherence, order and harmony—or real peace in the immediate environment. This environmental phenomenon is known as the Extended Maharishi Effect and will be discussed further on.

The Maharishi Effect

Scientific research has found that in cities and towns all over the world, when as little as one percent of the population practices the Transcendental Meditation technique, the trend of rising crime rate is reversed, indicating increasing order and harmony in the collective consciousness of the whole society.

Research scientists have named this phenomenon the Maharishi Effect, because this finding was the confirmation of Maharishi's promise to society made in Los Angeles in 1959 and even earlier in India.

The Extended Maharishi Effect

With the addition of the TM-Sidhi program and its speciality, Yogic Flying, scientists expected that the collective consciousness of a nation's society would be affected in a original way. The effect of peace would be the same, but the means to achieve it would differ. Scientists predicted that the square root of one percent of a population practicing the Transcendental Meditation technique and the TM-Sidhi program as a group, morning and evening in one place, would produce sufficient coherence to neutralize negative tendencies and promote positive trends throughout the population of the nation. This was called the Extended Maharishi Effect.

The first major test of this prediction took place in 1978 during Maharishi's Global Ideal Society Campaign in 108 countries: crime rate was reduced everywhere.

The Global Maharishi Effect

When the square root of one percent of the world's population (approximately 7000 Yogic Flyers) practice the Transcendental Meditation and TM-Sidhi programs together in a group, morning and evening in one place, the coherence-creating effect occurs on a global scale, reducing violence and negative trends world-wide.

An example of the Global Maharishi Effect occurred in 1981 when 7000 Yogic Flyers attended three large World Peace Assemblies over a period of two to three weeks in the U.S.A., the Netherlands and India. These Yogic Flyers enjoyed deep and pure bliss while creating coherence in collective consciousness, thereby generating a unifying and integrating effect in the life of the nation and world. As a result such negative trends as crime, accidents and sickness decreased while the world society enjoyed an increase in positive social, economic and political trends.

The secret of the Global Maharishi Effect is the phenomenon known to physics as the "field effect," the effect of coherence and positivity produced from the field of pure Transcendental Consciousness. Group practice of Yogic Flying demonstrates the field effect in that it unifies the functioning of the intelligence of different individuals with their differing values of physiology.

Veda and the Human Physiology:
The Most Advanced Vedic Technology

Inspired by Maharishi, a Harvard-trained medical doctor, Professor Tony Nader, M.D., Ph.D., has undertaken a fascinating voyage of discovery into the theoretical field of physiology as it relates to the literature of the ancient Veda. In his research, he has uncovered striking correspondences. According to Dr. Nader, the same Laws of Nature responsible for constructing the human mind and body also structure the syllables, verses, chapters and texts of the ancient Veda and Vedic Literature.

Dr. Nader's research has demonstrated that the human physiology (including DNA at its core) has the same structure and function as the holistic, self-sufficient, self-referral reality expressed in the fundamental book of Rik Veda. The specialized components, organs and organ systems of the human physiology, including all parts of the nervous system, match the 40 branches of the Vedic Literature, one to one, both in structure and function.

Dr. Nader points out that the study of physiology in terms of the structure of Veda is the revelation of our scientific age and raises the individual dignity of humans to the cosmic dignity of the universe. For Dr. Nader, the individual is the Cosmos in the truest sense. This discovery means that the inner administrator of our own life is the same as the administrator of the whole universe. Our own physiology is, in fact, the Vedic Literature in manifest form.

For more information on the relation of Veda to human physiology, you can read Dr. Nader's book: *Human Physiology: Expression of Veda and Vedic Literature.*

Appendix B **Notes**

1. (p. 66)

    The brain of man is equipped with the ability....

    Scientific research has confirmed that during the practice of the
    Transcendental Meditation technique cortical response to percep-
    tual stimuli increases. Also, the functional relationship existing
    between the two hemispheres of the brain improves. This means
    that a normal brain becomes more orderly, resulting in: enhanced
    creativity, increased efficiency of perception and memory, improved
    verbal and analytical thinking and improved synthetic and holistic
    thinking. Physiologically, we find increased stability of the auto-
    nomic nervous system, faster reactions, faster reflex responses and
    faster recovery from stress. *See charts on pages 220 & 221.*

2. (p. 74)

    ...the gains possible with the Transcendental Meditation program.

    Scientific research shows that during the practice of the Tran-
    scendental Meditation technique, an individual experiences pro-
    found relaxation and deep rest, as indicated by greater decreases in
    respiration rates and plasma lactate levels compared to ordinary

rest. Along with this rest comes increased EEG coherence, increased blood flow to the brain and increased efficiency of information transfer in the brain, indicating stronger mind/body coordination. Other research shows increased development of intelligence and increased self-actualization, characteristics of a stronger mind. *See charts, pages 219 & 220.*

3. (p. 75)
...war would be an impossibility.
Over 50 scientific research studies have confirmed that when one percent of a social population practices the Maharishi Transcendental Meditation program in a group, crime rates plummet and positive social indicators rise. This phenomenon is called the Maharishi Effect.

Furthermore, when the square root of one percent of a social population, such as a city, a nation or even the world as a whole, practices the Maharishi Transcendental Meditation program along with its more advanced technology, the TM-Sidhi program with its specialty—Yogic Flying, in a group, such a powerful influence of coherence and harmony gets innocently created that urban crime and social conflicts and violence automatically decrease. Even war intensity and war deaths drop dramatically. Along with these welcomed decreases come increased progress towards resolution of conflicts, and an improved quality of city, state, national and international life. *See charts, pages 233, 234 & 235.*

4. (p. 82)
...meditation made me tolerate them a little better.
Regular practice of the Transcendental Meditation technique

leads to decreased anxiety, increased tolerance, decreased hostility and improved orientation towards positive values. *See chart, page 228.*

5. (p. 111)
    It strengthened us through the strange situation that we were in.
    The Maharishi Transcendental Meditation technique significantly increases our ability to remain focused on the task at hand and to not get distracted. This ability would help anyone get "through strange situations." The Transcendental Meditation technique also significantly increases self-actualization—the ability to realize our own inner potential in every area of life. This means that we remain true to our goals, regardless of what others think or say. Other studies show an increase in self-development and self-confidence. This means that our thoughts and actions become more nourishing and progressive for ourselves and others as we innocently practice the technique. That's why my mother could say that the Transcendental Meditation technique strengthened her through the strange situation she was in. *See chart, page 224.*

6. (p. 111)
    ...younger, happier and more relaxed.
    Scientists have confirmed that regular practice of the Transcendental Meditation technique reverses the aging process. In one particular study, scientists looked at biological age and compared it to chronological age. Long-term practitioners were physiologically 12 years younger than their chronological age. In addition, the Transcendental Meditation technique increases relaxation and allows us to experience the source of happiness within, a state of

pure bliss consciousness. That brief experience of bliss can result in increased happiness during daily life activities. *See charts, pages 219 & 227.*

7. (p. 111)
    ...less strained and worried....
    Regular practice of the Transcendental Meditation technique outperforms other types of stress management techniques such as concentration-based or contemplation-based technologies for reducing trait anxiety. It also leads to faster recovery from stress, increased capacity for warm interpersonal relations, increased resistance to distraction and social pressure, reduced job worry and tension, and greater marital satisfaction and adjustment. *See charts, pages 224 & 220.*

8. (p. 112)
    ...shift of values....
    Higher levels of moral maturity have been noted among practitioners of the Transcendental Meditation technique, along with increased self-confidence and self-actualization. *See chart, page 224.*

9. (p. 147)
    ...fulfillment to education.
    Maharishi has introduced to the world, through his schools and universities, a Vedic system of education that offers both knowledge and experience of the highest value of human life. Students show a greater interest in academic activities and are blessed with improved memory as well as greater creativity. Academic achievements come easily to any Maharishi School

student, and university graduates come away equipped to handle the fast pace of today's busy society. School violence is practically unknown at any Maharishi school or university. *See charts, pages 221, 222 & 223.*

10. (p. 161)

One day...smoking was no longer a part of life.

Smokers who learn the Transcendental Meditation technique may find a significant decrease in their smoking habits without experiencing the anxiety that normally accompanies symptomatic withdrawal from addictive behaviors. It happens automatically, without trying. *See chart, page 229.*

11. (p. 163)

All is bliss; omnipresent is the Kingdom of Heaven.

See Appendix E for the complete lecture that Maharishi gave at the University of Southern California.

12. (p. 164)

...if the people in jails could be taught the Transcendental Meditation program....

Scientific research confirms reduced recidivism for those felons who practice the Transcendental Meditation technique. Research also shows a decrease in prison rule violations, decreased hostility, decreased drug abuse and a greater number of clean parole records. Several court judges in the Midwest now sentence certain lawbreakers to practice the Transcendental Meditation technique, with amazingly good and lasting results. Maybe this could be a way to empty our jails by bringing inner fulfillment to felons and thereby changing their need to commit crimes to create temporary outer fulfillment. *See chart, page 232.*

13. (p. 165)

...juvenile delinquency....

Research demonstrates significant improvements for juvenile offenders who practice the Transcendental Meditation program regularly. Meditating juvenile offenders have decreased court problems, decreased anxiety and show greater positive changes as reported by subjects and parents. If juveniles practiced the Transcendental Meditation program perhaps the need for school violence would decrease if not disappear altogether. *See chart, page 232.*

14. (p. 165)

...would it not be possible to suppose that we could arrive at an ideal state, a "Utopia"?

Utopia means an ideal society. Scientific studies repeatedly show that increased coherence in the collective consciousness of a society develops through the Maharishi Effect. As the quality of life improves, that society comes closer to reflecting those characteristics descriptive of an ideal society. In fact, based on these scientific findings, in 1977 Maharishi inaugurated a global campaign to create ideal societies in 108 countries. The campaign is still underway. *See charts, pages 233 & 234.*

15. (p. 167)

Businessmen like to stress the value of the Transcendental Meditation technique.

For those business people who practice the Transcendental Meditation technique, job worry and tension decrease; work and personal relationships at work improve; job performance and job satisfaction are enhanced. A meditating work force enjoys increased creativity, improved problem-solving ability, and improved physiological stability during task performance. *See charts, pages 230 & 231.*

16. (p. 167)

...health improved because tensions were released from the body.

Quite a bit of research documents the health benefits that accrue from regular practice of the Maharishi Transcendental Meditation technique including: decreased hospitalization and doctor visits, decreased blood pressure, decreased serum cholesterol levels, healthier response to stress, and increased longevity. *See charts, pages 225 & 226.*

17. (p. 168)

...the world could be at peace....

Now known as the global Maharishi Effect, scientific research shows that when **the square root of one percent** of the world's population (approximately 7000 people) participate in group practice of the Transcendental Meditation and TM-Sidhi programs and Yogic Flying, international conflicts decrease, global positivity increases and global economic prosperity results.

World peace can become a lasting reality in this generation;

all we have to do is devote a significantly tiny portion of our daily activity to the practice of this marvelously simple procedure and then go about our normal routine. Just a little practice to ensure a world worthwhile to live in; is it too much to ask? *See chart, page 235.*

18. (p. 179)

Read about *"The most constructive program for world peace known so far to the civilized world"* in Appendix D, the Three Year Plan of the Spiritual Regeneration Movement 1960-1962.

19. (p. 203)

For thousands of people, the Transcendental Meditation technique is "a non-medicinal tranquilizer." It readily removes mental tensions and does away with the very cause of psychosomatic ailments. *See charts, pages 219, 228 & 229.*

20. (p. 204)

Presently, over 600 scientific studies conducted at more than 200 universities and research institutions in thirty countries demonstrate the profound benefits of the Transcendental Meditation and TM-Sidhi programs for mind, body, behavior and environment. Scientific laboratories located at Maharishi universities world-wide continue rigorous investigation into the benefits of Maharishi's Vedic technologies for all areas of life.

Appendix C Scientific Charts

Physiological Indicators of Deep Rest
Through the **Transcendental Meditation** Technique

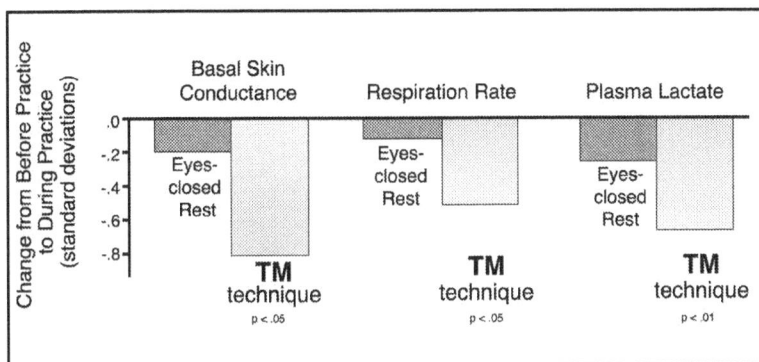

A meta-analysis (used for drawing objective conclusions from large bodies of research) found that the Transcendental Meditation technique produced a significant decrease in basal skin conductance compared to eyes-closed rest, indicating profound relaxation. Deep rest and relaxation were also indicated by greater decreases in respiration rates and plasma lactate levels compared to ordinary rest. These physiological changes occur spontaneously as the mind effortlessly settles to the state of restful alertness, Transcendental Consciousness.

References:
1. *American Psychologist 42* (1987): 879–881.
2. *Science 167* (1970): 1751–1754.
3. *American Journal of Physiology 221* (1971): 795–799.

Mobilization of the Latent Reserves of the Brain
Through the **Transcendental Meditation** Technique

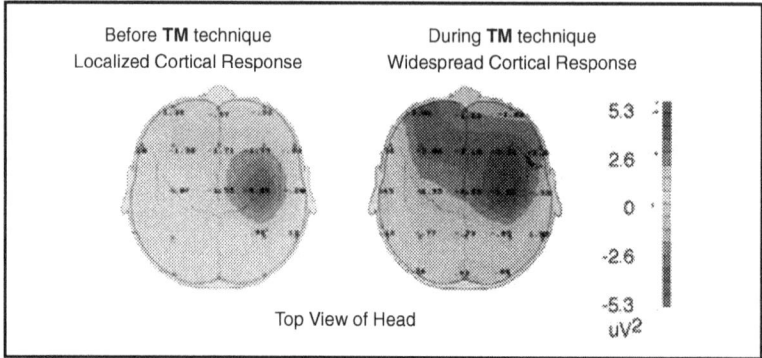

Before **TM** technique
Localized Cortical Response

During **TM** technique
Widespread Cortical Response

5.3
2.6
0
-2.6
-5.3
uV²

Top View of Head

This study found that during the Transcendental Meditation program some of the early sensory components of the brain's response to somatosensory stimulation (0–100 msec) are more widely distributed across the cortex. This study, by Dr. Nicolai Nicolaevich Lyubimov, Director of the Moscow Brain Research Institute's Laboratory of Neurocybernetics, indicates that during the Transcendental Meditation program there is an increase in the areas of the cortex taking part in perception of specific information and an increase in the functional relationship between the two hemispheres.

References:
1. Proceedings of the International Symposium *Physiological and Biochemical Basis of Brain Activity*, St. Petersburg, Russia, (June 22–24, 1994).
2. 2nd Russian-Swedish Symposium *New Research in Neurobiology*, Moscow, Russia (May 19–21, 1992).

Optimization of Brain Functioning
Through the **Transcendental Meditation** Technique

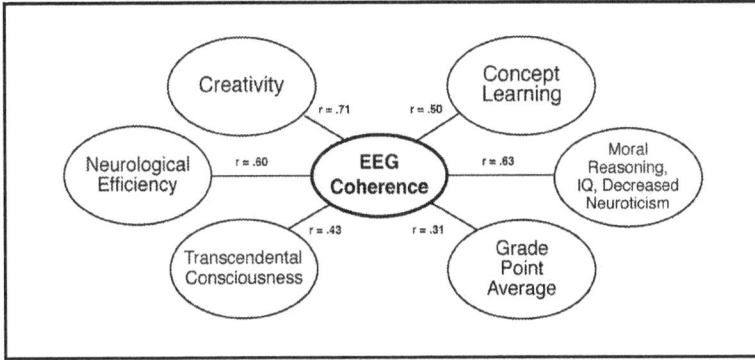

Higher levels of **EEG** coherence measured during the practice of the Transcendental Meditation technique are significantly correlated with increased fluency of verbal creativity, increased efficiency in learning new concepts, more principled moral reasoning, higher verbal IQ, decreased neuroticism, higher academic achievement, clearer experiences of Transcendental Consciousness, and increased neurological efficiency, as measured by faster recovery of the H-reflex.

References:
The chart above was constructed with data from the following four studies:

1. *International Journal of Neuroscience 13* (1981): 211–217.
2. *International Journal of Neuroscience 15* (1981): 151–157.
3. *Scientific Research on the* Transcendental Meditation *Program: Collected Papers, Volume 1* (1977): 208–212.
4. *Scientific Research on the* Transcendental Meditation *and* TM-Sidhi *Programme: Collected Papers, Volume 4* (1989): 2245–2266.

Development of Intelligence–Increased IQ

Through the **Transcendental Meditation** Technique

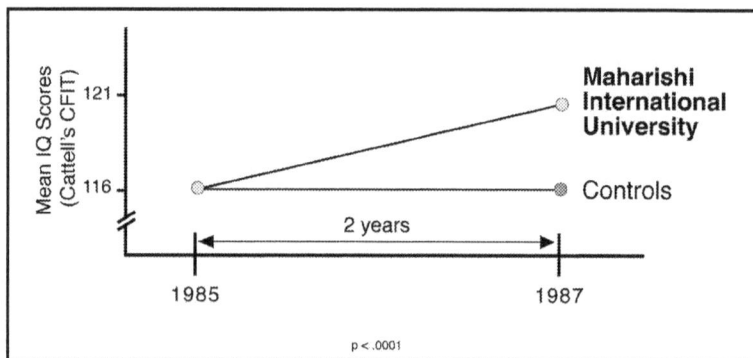

Students at Maharishi International University (now Maharishi University of Management) in Fairfield, Iowa, U.S.A., who regularly practiced the Transcendental Meditation and TM-Sidhi programs over a two-year period, increased significantly in intelligence and in the ability to make rapid choice decisions compared to control subjects from another Iowa university. This finding corroborates other studies showing increased IQ and faster choice reaction through practice of the Transcendental Meditation technique.

References:

1. *Personality and Individual Differences 12* (1991): 1105–1116.
2. *Perceptual and Motor Skills 62* (1986): 731–738.
3. *College Student Journal 15* (1981): 140–146.
4. *The Journal of Creative Behavior 19* (1985): 270–275.
5. *Journal of Clinical Psychology 42* (1986): 161–164.
6. *Gedrag: Tijdschrift voor Psychologie [Behavior: Journal of Psychology] 3* (1975): 167–182.

Improved Academic Performance
Through the **Transcendental Meditation** Technique

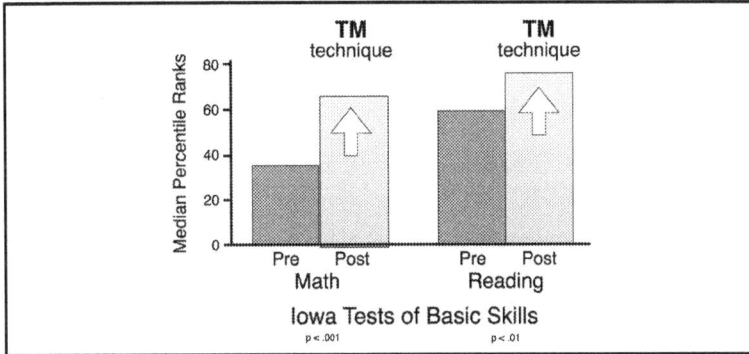

After one year of practice of the Transcendental Meditation program, elementary school students showed significant gains on the Iowa Tests of Basic Skills, a nationally standardized test (ref. 1). A second study showed significant gains in high school students (grades 9–12) on the Iowa Tests of Educational Development (ref. 2). A third study (ref. 3) found that the length of time students had been practicing the Transcendental Meditation program was significantly correlated with academic achievement, independent of student IQ scores.

References:
1. *Education 107* (1986): 49–54.
2. *Education 109* (1989): 302–304.
3. *Modern Science and Vedic Science 1* (1987): 433–468.

Increased Self-Actualization

Through the **Transcendental Meditation** Technique

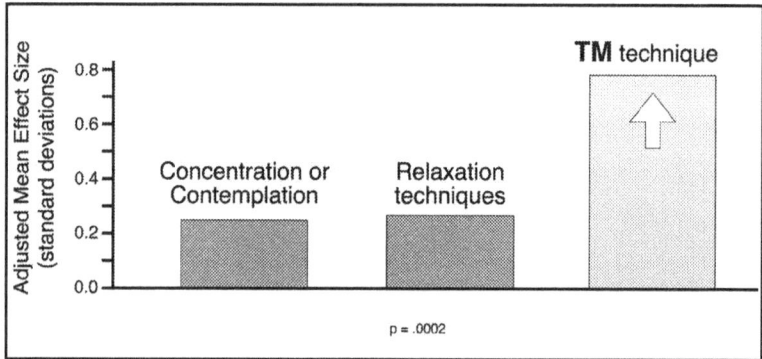

Statistical meta-analysis of all available studies (42 independent outcomes) indicated that the effect of the Transcendental Meditation program on increasing self-actualization is much greater than concentration, contemplation, or relaxation techniques. Self-actualization refers to realizing more of one's inner potential, expressed in every area of life: integration and stability of personality, self-regard, emotional maturity, capacity for warm interpersonal relationships, and adaptive response to challenges.

References:

1. *Journal of Social Behavior and Personality 6* (1991): 189–247.
2. *Journal of Counseling Psychology 19* (1972): 184–187.
3. *Higher Stages of Human Development: Perspectives on Adult Growth* (New York: Oxford University Press, 1990), 286–341.

Decreased Hospitalization and Doctor Visits
Through the **Transcendental Meditation** Technique

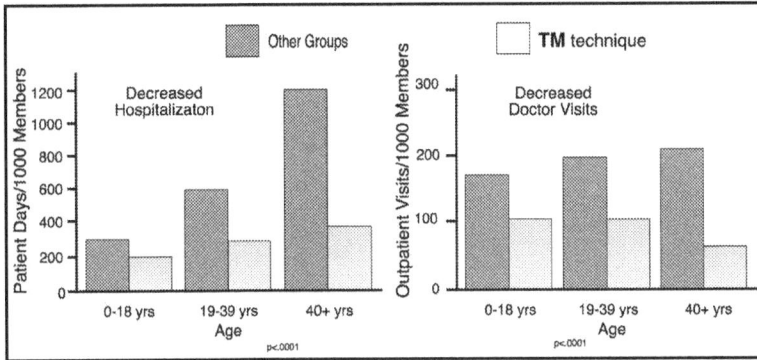

A five-year study of medical care utilization statistics on 2,000 people throughout the U.S.A. who regularly practiced the Transcendental Meditation program found that their overall rate of hospitalization was 56% lower than the norm. The group practicing the Transcendental Meditation technique had fewer hospital admissions in all disease categories compared to the norm— including 87% less hospitalization for cardiovascular disease, 55% less for cancer, 87% less for diseases of the nervous system, and 73% less for nose, throat, and lung problems.

References:
1. *Psychosomatic Medicine 49* (1987): 493–507.
2. *American Journal of Health Promotion*, 10 (1996): 208–216.

Decreased Health Care Expenditures
Through the **Transcendental Meditation** Technique

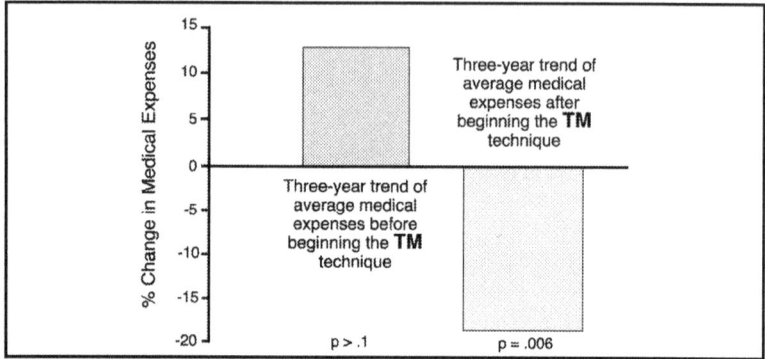

This chart shows three-year averages of medical expenses for physicians' services of participants before and after practice of the Transcendental Meditation program. In this study, government payments for physicians' services (approximately 20% of total medical expenses) were examined for 677 Quebec health plan enrollees who learned the Transcendental Meditation program. During the three years prior to beginning the Transcendental Meditation program, subjects' expenses (adjusted for inflation, age, and gender) did not change significantly. After learning the Transcendental Meditation program, subjects' adjusted expenses declined significantly, by 5–7% annually.

References:
1. *American Journal of Health Promotion* (1996, in press).
2. *Psychosomatic Medicine 49* (1987):493–507.
3. *Journal of the Iowa Academy of Science 95* (1)(1988): A56.

Reversal of the Aging Process
Through the **Transcendental Meditation** Technique

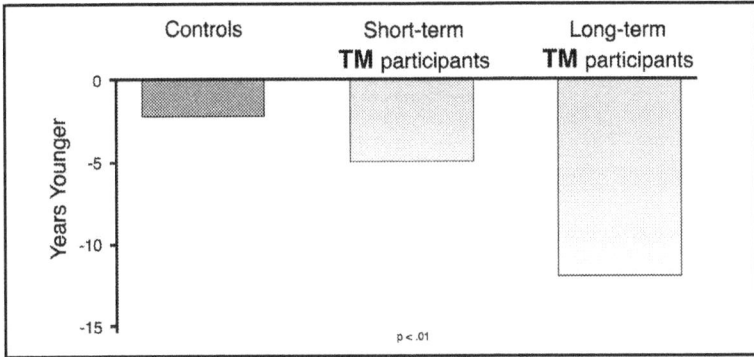

The Transcendental Meditation technique is a major component of the Maharishi Vedic Approach to Health[SM]. This study examined the effect of the Transcendental Meditation program on what researchers in the field of aging have called the "biological age" of a person—how old a person is physiologically in contrast to chronologically. As a group, long-term TM program participants, who had been practicing the Transcendental Meditation program for more than five years, were physiologically 12 years younger than their chronological age, as measured by lower blood pressure, better near-point vision, and better auditory discrimination. Short-term TM program participants were physiologically 5 years younger than their chronological age. The study statistically controlled for the effects of diet and exercise.

References:
1. *International Journal of Neuroscience 16* (1982): 53–58.
2. *Journal of Personality and Social Psychology 57* (1989): 950–964.
3. *Journal of Behavioral Medicine* (1986): 327–334.

Reduced Anxiety
Through the **Transcendental Meditation** Technique

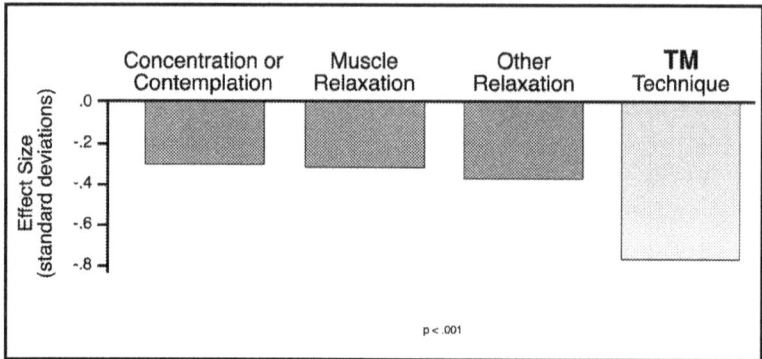

Concentration or Contemplation | Muscle Relaxation | Other Relaxation | **TM** Technique

Effect Size (standard deviations)

.0
-.2
-.4
-.6
-.8

p < .001

A statistical meta-analysis conducted at Stanford University of all available studies (146 independent outcomes) indicated that the effect of the Transcendental Meditation program on reducing trait anxiety was much greater than that of concentration and contemplation or forms of physical relaxation, including muscle relaxation. Analysis showed that these positive results could not be attributed to subject expectation, experimenter bias, or quality of research design.

References:
1. *Journal of Clinical Psychology 45* (1989): 957–974.
2. *Journal of Clinical Psychology 33* (1977): 1076–1078.

Reduced Drug and Alcohol Use
Through the **Transcendental Meditation** Technique

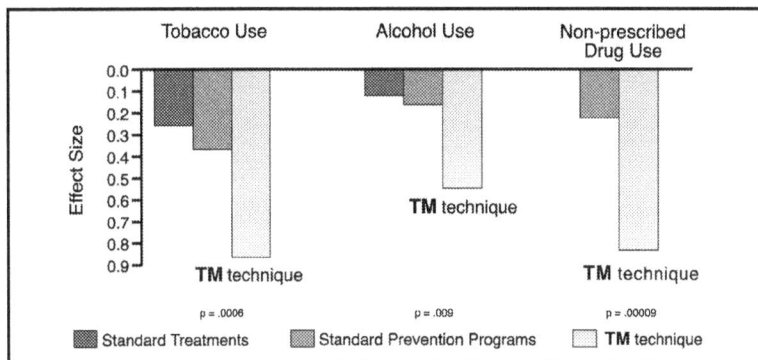

A statistical meta-analysis of 198 independent treatment outcomes found that the Transcendental Meditation program produced a significantly larger reduction in tobacco, alcohol, and non-prescribed drug use than standard substance abuse treatments and standard prevention programs. Whereas the effects of conventional programs typically fall off rapidly within three months, effects of the Transcendental Meditation program increase over time, with total abstinence from tobacco, alcohol, and non-prescribed drugs ranging from 51%-89% over a 18-22 month period. The effects of the Transcendental Meditation program are based on fundamental and naturally occurring improvements in the individuals' psychophysiological functioning.

References:
1. *Alcoholism Treatment Quarterly 11* (1994): 13–87.
2 *International Journal of the Addictions 26* (1991): 293–325.
3. *Self Recovery: Treating Addictions Using Transcendental Meditation and Maharishi Ayur-Veda. The Haworth Press, New York* (1994).

Improved Health Among the Work Force
Through the **Transcendental Meditation** Technique

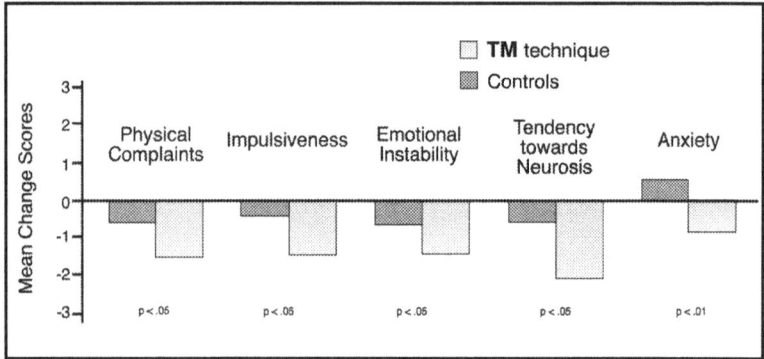

In a large study conducted over a five-month period by the National Institute of Industrial Health of the Japanese Ministry of Labor and the St. Marianna Medical Institute, 447 industrial workers of Sumitomo Heavy Industries were taught the Transcendental Meditation technique and compared with 321 workers who did not learn the Transcendental Meditation technique. The Transcendental Meditation technique group showed significantly decreased physical complaints, decreased impulsiveness, decreased emotional instability, decreased neurotic tendencies, decreased anxiety, and decreased insomnia.

References:

1. *Japanese Journal of Industrial Health 32* (1990): 656.
2. *Japanese Journal of Public Health 37* (1990): 729.

Enhanced Job Performance and Job Satisfaction

Through the **Transcendental Meditation** Technique

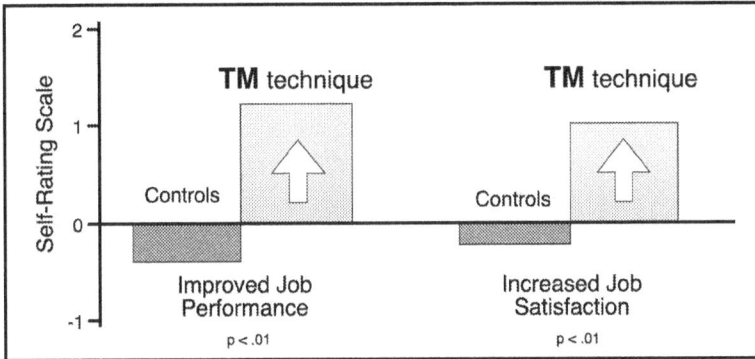

Employees practicing the Transcendental Meditation program an average of 11 months showed significant improvements at work compared with members of a control group. Relationships with co-workers and supervisors improved, and job performance and job satisfaction increased, while the desire to change jobs decreased (ref. 1). The results of this research were replicated in a study with several control groups, which also found significant improvements in the same areas (ref. 2).

References:

1. *Academy of Management Journal 17* (1974): 362–368.
2. *Scientific Research on the* Transcendental Meditation *Program: Collected Papers, Volume 1* (1977): 630–638.
3. *Anxiety, Stress, and Coping: An International Journal 6* (1993): 245–262.

Reduced Recidivism
Through the **Transcendental Meditation** Technique

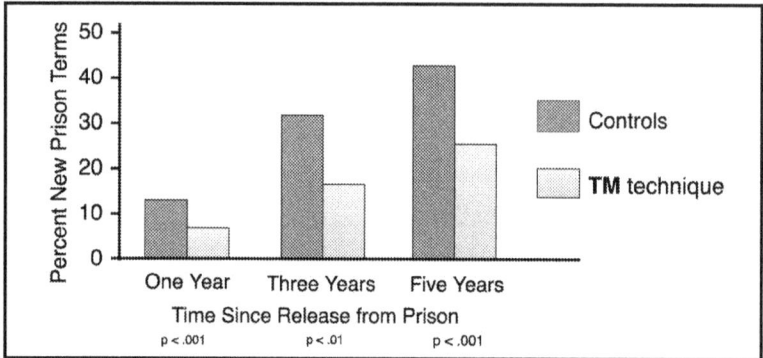

In this study, 259 male felon parolees of the California Depart-ment of Corrections who learned the Transcendental Meditation technique while in prison had fewer new prison terms and more favorable parole outcomes each year over a five-year period after release compared to carefully matched controls. The Transcen-dental Meditation program was shown to significantly reduce recidivism during a period of six months to six years after parole, whereas prison education, vocational training, and psychotherapy did not consistently reduce recidivism.

References:

1. *Journal of Criminal Justice 15* (1987): 211–230.
2. *Dissertation Abstracts International 43* (1982): 539B.
3. *International Journal of Comparative and Applied Criminal Justice 11* (1987): 111–132.

Maharishi Effect:
Increased Orderliness, Decreased Urban Crime
Through Group Practice of the
Transcendental Meditation and **TM-Sidhi** Programs

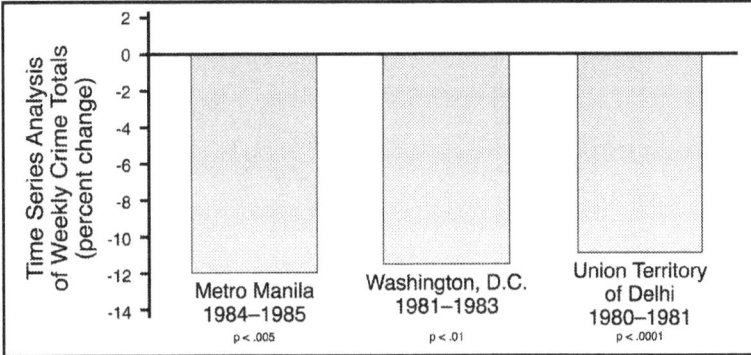

During periods when groups practicing the Transcendental Meditation and TM-Sidhi programs exceeded the square root of one percent of the population, crime decreased in Metro Manila, Philippines (mid-August 1984 to late January 1985); Washington, D.C. (October 1981 to October 1983); and the Union Territory of Delhi, India (November 1980 to March 1981). Time series analysis verified that these decreases in crime could not have been due to trends or cycles of crime, or to changes in police policies and procedures.

References:
1. *The Journal of Mind and Behavior 8* (1987): 67–104.
2. *The Journal of Mind and Behavior 9* (1988): 457–486.

233

Global Maharishi Effect: Improved Quality of Life and Reduced Conflict in the Middle East

Through Group Practice of the
Transcendental Meditation and **TM-Sidhi** Programs

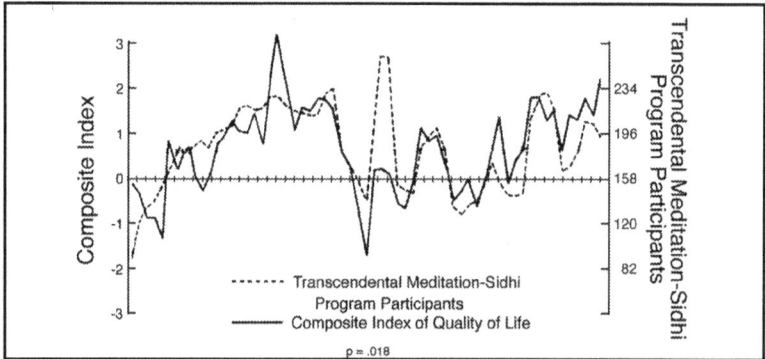

This study indicates that group practice of the Maharishi Transcendental Meditation and TM-Sidhi programs improved the quality of life in Israel as measured by improvement on an index consisting of reduced crime rate, reduced traffic accidents, reduced fires, the reduced number of war deaths in Lebanon, increases in the national stock market, and improvements in national mood. The chart above shows the strong correspondence between the number of Transcendental Meditation-Sidhi program participants in the group in Jerusalem and a composite index of all the above variables.

References:
1. *Journal of Conflict Resolution 32* (1988): 776–812.
2. *Dissertation Abstracts International 4* (1988): 2381A.

Global Maharishi Effect:
Increased Positivity and Reduced International Conflict
Through Group Practice of the
Transcendental Meditation and **TM-Sidhi** Programs

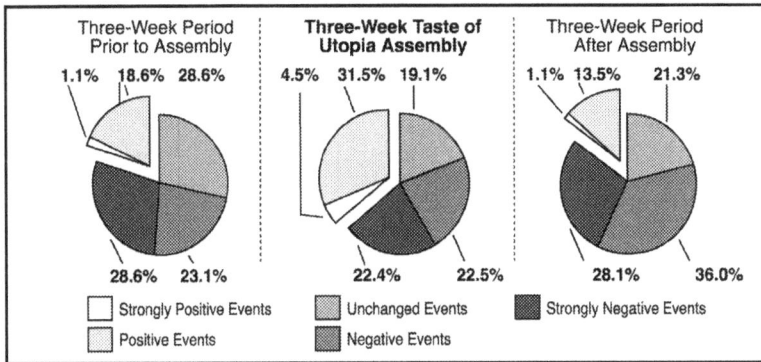

In the winter of 1983–84, a group of 7,000 TM-Sidhi program Yogic Flyers assembled at Maharishi University of Management in Iowa to create world peace (the Taste of Utopia Assembly). During the assembly a content analysis of articles reporting international conflict showed a significant shift towards greater positivity and reduced conflict compared to before the assembly. After the assembly, international events reverted to their prior level of conflict.

Reference:
Scientific Research on the Transcendental Meditation *and* TM-Sidhi *Program: Collected Papers, Volume 4* (1989).

235

Appendix D **Three Year Plan**
of the Spiritual Regeneration Movement 1960-1962

Editor's Note:

The Three Year Plan of the Spiritual Regeneration Movement, which Maharishi created in 1959, has served as his basic theme for the expansion of the TM Movement. Maharishi has since offered a second Three Year Plan, a Five Year Plan for students, and the World Plan of the '70s. In 1976 he founded the World Government of the Age of Enlightenment having ten ministries whose goals were to fulfill the basic premises of his original Three Year Plan.

During the 1980s Maharishi formulated Vedic systems of Education, Health, Government, Economics, Defense, Rehabilitation and Agriculture in order to create an ideal civilization. He also presented a World Plan for Perfect Health whose aim was to create a disease-free society through the implementation of the Maharishi Vedic Approach to Health throughout the world. And, in 1988 Maharishi inaugurated a Master Plan to Create Heaven on Earth.

The 1990s focused on the development of Global Administration through Natural Law. During this decade Maharishi created a new structure for administering his global TM Movement by establishing twelve Time-Zone Capitals around the world. According to Maharishi, each Capital will administer to the needs of the Maharishi Vedic Centers, universities, and Ayur-Vedic facilities located in that time zone. Each Capital will be housed in one of the tallest buildings in that time zone, constructed according to Vedic principles of architecture. The Time-Zone Capital^{SM} building will allow for the proper number of Yogic Flyers to practice the Transcendental Meditation and TM-Sidhi programs together as a group and thus perpetuate ideal life in that time zone.

In 1999, Maharishi inaugurated the first country of world peace near Brazil. His vision presented in the original Three Year Plan became reality at the end of the twentieth century.

Reprinted here are the relevant sections of the original Three Year Plan.

TO THE BOUNDLESS RESOURCES OF INNER MAN

The Highway to World Peace
THREE YEAR PLAN
of the
SPIRITUAL REGENERATION MOVEMENT
1960 – 1962

The Spiritual Regeneration Movement aims at universal peace and harmony through the development of peace and harmony in the life of the individual. The unique feature of this worldwide movement, which distinguishes it completely from other movements of similar aim, is that it offers something of practical value.

It brings to the door of the busy, worldly man a key to the unfoldment of higher consciousness—a simple practice of meditation which enables everyone to enjoy peace of mind, inner happiness, increased ability, and proper sense of values in all walks of life.

PHILOSOPHY OF THE MOVEMENT

Life is bliss, essentially it is not a struggle.

Man is born to enjoy, certainly not to suffer.

Man is born of bliss, of consciousness, of wisdom, and creativity.

All this is found in fullness when the flower of life blooms in full—the blossoming of all glories, inner and outer.
When the inner spiritual and outer material glories of life are

consciously harmonized, the life becomes integrated and such a life is worth living.

Life has two aspects—Inner and outer.

Inner life is absolute bliss consciousness.
It is unconditioned, eternal existence, happiness, wisdom, and creativity.

Outer life is relative.
It is existence, happiness, wisdom, and creativity conditioned by time, space, and causation.

The inner sphere of life is the source of the outer.
It is the fountainhead of the outer spring of life.

Direct connection and harmony with the inner life is the basis of all glories of the outer life in the world.
Everyone's mind is always searching for greater happiness.
When it is rightly turned inwards, it enjoys the inner glories spontaneously.

No controlling of the mind is necessary, and no long and strenuous practices are necessary to lead the mind inwards.
In the inward direction lies the ocean of happiness, the bliss of the absolute, which is enough to attract the mind in a natural way and enable man to express the inner glory of life in all the practical aspects of life.

No withdrawal from responsibilities of life is needed to integrate one's life and to live fullness of life in the world.

It is wrong to believe that wandering is the nature of the mind.
The mind is found wandering only to settle down somewhere in bliss. Not finding anything charming to rest on, it begins to feel miserable. This establishes that wandering is not the nature of the mind. Therefore, all advantages of controlling the mind can easily be gained by leading the mind to the blissful field of inner life and satisfying its thirst for happiness.

Maharishi's simple system of transcendental meditation is a technique based on the natural tendency of the mind to go to a medium of greater happiness.
Therefore, it is easy for everyone to enjoy all advantages of the unfoldment of higher consciousness through this practice.

Maharishi's system of transcendental meditation easily harmonizes the inner and outer glories of life.
It is a golden link to connect the material and the spiritual values of existence.

Furthermore—it not only establishes harmony between the material and spiritual aspects of life but directly enhances the glories of material life by the light of the spiritual experience; and this is the uniqueness of this system suited to the fast materialistic tempo of modern living.

Thousands all over the world have experienced that it is so.

On the basis of personal experience of the people and with their help, the movement is spreading fast to reach everyone, everywhere.

AND THIS HAS
GIVEN RISE TO
THE THREE YEAR PLAN

INTRODUCTION TO THE THREE YEAR PLAN
by John Smith Hislop, M.A., Ed.D.
Los Angeles, California

THE THREE YEAR PLAN of the Spiritual Regeneration Movement is the most constructive program for world peace known so far to the civilized world. It aims at universal peace and harmony through the development of peace and harmony in the life of the individual. It is a systematic drive to bring to each and all the maximum advantage of the Spiritual Regeneration Movement which aims at spiritual awakening to neutralize disharmony and tension in all walks of human life.

BASIC PRINCIPLE

The basic principle of this worldwide movement is that every man has a tremendous amount of energy and potentiality latent in him, and that every one has the basic ability to discover and use this great treasure present within himself. With such a natural gift, there is no reason for man to suffer in any way. But man is found suffering. He suffers in many ways ONLY due to ignorance of how to discover his inner potentialities and use them with advantage in daily life. Unaware of the technique of unfolding the inner consciousness, man is found suffering in life. All human suffering could be eliminated by educating man in the art of unfolding his own inner consciousness and helping him to realize his own real nature free from all shortcomings.

MAN DOES NEED HELP

Do men need help to find the treasure, that is their own, to find the glory of their own consciousness? The records show that men do need help. A Christ, a Buddha, a Krishna enters the world to lead men to salvation. Certain men in all centuries rise to unity with the Divine, and men call them "Master" or "Guru" and beseech them to show the way to eternal happiness. Religions arise because man cries for help to get out of his misery and find everlasting joy.

WHERE?

Where is there such a teacher today? Where, today, is there a great spiritual leader who can directly show men an open way to eternal freedom?

I say there is such a man abroad in the world today. Maharishi Mahesh Yogi makes no claim of status for himself. He only says that he knows a way for every person of normal mind to dive deep within himself, find the source of energy, peace and happiness, and achieve the ultimate purpose of life. He only says that it is his aim to show every man and woman how to be free from the worries and tensions of daily life, how to be free from misery and bondage. He only says that his aim is to spiritually regenerate humanity and establish lasting peace and happiness in the world.

SUBLIME EPISODE OF HISTORY

Despite his refusal to make any claim of status for himself, Maharishi Mahesh Yogi is destined to become one of history's great spiritual leaders. His crusade to spiritually regenerate all of humanity through the direct and quick path of Transcendental Meditation is one of the sublime episodes of history. One man from India setting out to change the course of the world and establish universal peace and happiness! To such a man, to such an ideal, to such a holy crusade, I drop on bended knee in admiration and homage, and I pledge my assistance to the fullest possible extent.

HISTORY OF THE MOVEMENT

The Spiritual Regeneration Movement was started by His Holiness Maharishi Mahesh Yogi in January, 1958, in Madras, India, when the SEMINAR OF SPIRITUAL LUMINARIES was held to celebrate the 89th Birthday Anniversary of the great Spiritual Master His Divinity Swami Brahmananda Saraswati Jagadguru Shankaracharya of Jyotir Math, Himalayas.

By the end of the first year, the wave of the Spiritual Regeneration Movement reached across the Pacific halfway around the world and created a stir in the spiritual understanding of America. The modem message of ancient India was heard in the discourses of Maharishi Mahesh Yogi, who declared, "It is not difficult to experience the inner glory of the Divine even for a busy modern man." He declared it theoretically, proved it logically, scientifically, and practically by guiding people to experience it.

MEDITATION

According to Maharishi, meditation means the directing of the attention inward toward the subtle levels of the ocean of mind until the ultimate level of life is attained, and the source of limitless energy, peace and bliss is gained.

A SIMPLE TECHNIQUE

Maharishi has developed a simple technique of Transcendental Meditation by which all the levels of higher consciousness are rapidly reached. The tremendous potentialities of the inner self are thereby utilized to unfold latent capacities for all achievement in the field of thought and action.

UNIQUENESS

Maharishi's simple system of Transcendental Meditation is unique, because it has outmoded traditional methods of meditation as practiced not only in the West but also in the East. According to Maharishi:

1. *Everyone has the capacity for Transcendental Meditation.*

2. *No special power of concentration on the part of the meditator is required.*

3. *It requires no withdrawal or departure from the normal activities of daily life.*

4. *Only a few minutes of daily practice are necessary to enjoy its results.*

5. *Its effects are directly experienced from the start.*

6. *Neither study nor any preparation is required to start and obtain sustained results.*

7. *It is completely free from hypnotism or spiritualism.*

FIRST INTERNATIONAL CONVENTION

The First International Convention of the Spiritual Regeneration Movement was of deep significance. It gave rise to the Three Year Plan at Sequoia National Park in California in July, 1959, and symbolized man's perfect dream and noble aspiration for good will and peace for the world. Let us rise to decide in our heart that we will do our utmost to help Maharishi Mahesh Yogi for the grand success of the THREE YEAR PLAN. No action that we can ever do will have a greater and more virtuous effect both on the world and on ourselves.

THREE YEAR PLAN 1960–1962

The main aim of the THREE YEAR PLAN is to set up a sound foundation and start a bold constructive program to accomplish the spiritual regeneration of the whole world as soon as possible.

Spiritual Regeneration of the world means progression of peace, harmony and happiness, and development of potentialities in every sphere of man's life: individual, social, national and international. This is to release all men from the worries, confusion, disharmony and suffering of day-to-day living, and to create a natural state of universal peace and harmony.

To accomplish this, the THREE YEAR PLAN aims at establishing 25,000 Meditation Centers all over the world.

These Meditation Centers will be sanctuaries of complete regeneration for man, for a harmonious development of his body, mind and soul. In modern language, these Meditation Centers will be the centers to advance the study of science, art and technology in the inner spheres of life, in the study of consciousness.

These Meditation Centers will educate the people in the art of unfolding the glories of inner life, and in the practical technique of Maharishi's simple system of Transcendental Meditation whereby every man of normal mind can easily unfold higher levels of consciousness, realize lasting peace and inner happiness, and develop latent faculties to gain more energy and ability in every walk of life.

With this is, life on earth will cease to be a struggle. All will experience *"LIFE IS BLISS."*

Progress in every sphere will be more profound, and the world will be in a natural state of peace and harmony.

The task of establishing 25,000 Meditation Centers all over the world within the three year time will be accomplished in a very systematic way.

Teachers of Transcendental Meditation will be trained under the direct guidance of His Holiness Maharishi Mahesh Yogi. They will establish these Meditation Centers and will function as Meditation Guides in their respective areas.

ACHIEVEMENT OF THE THREE YEAR PLAN

By the end of the Three Year Plan, the world will have about 25,000 trained Meditation Guides directing 25,000 Meditation Centers in different countries.

By this time interest will have been created in the public and about one tenth of the adult population of the civilized world will be practicing and enjoying the great gains of Maharishi's simple system of Transcendental Meditation.

This will really be the first major accomplishment of the Spiritual Regeneration Movement.

Maharishi is of great conviction that two more Three Year Plans based on this foundation will be sufficient to spiritually regenerate the whole world.

INTERNATIONAL ACADEMY OF MEDITATION

On the bank of the holy river Ganges in the Valley of Saints at Uttar-Kashi, in the heart of the Himalayan mountains of India, this sanctuary will be established to function as the main training center and the lighthouse of the Spiritual Regeneration Movement.

It will combine the comforts of modem living and the sanctity and serenity of the Himalayan caves of ancient India. This will be a place ideally suited to the seekers of truth. 84 Meditation Caves, constructed separately, at distances from one another, will have rooms built above them in which the students will live. With the modern facilities of communication and living, the International Academy of Meditation will also have a lecture hall and a library.

TRAINING IN THE
INTERNATIONAL ACADEMY OF MEDITATION

The training of Meditation Guides will comprise the following:

1. *Practical training in the art of Maharishi's simple system of Transcendental Meditation.*

2. *Theoretical training about the ideology of Transcendental Meditation, its various aspects—simplicity, universality, effectiveness, and*

far-reaching results, and also its relationship with different branches of learning, schools of philosophy and religions of the world.

3. *Study of the potentialities of Transcendental Meditation to harmonize the material and spiritual values of life.*

4. *Training in the art of guiding others in the practice of Transcendental Meditation.*

5. *Theoretical and practical training in different methods for developing perfect health.*

6. *Theoretical and practical training in methods of removing the mental blocks, worries and tensions of the people.*

7. *Training in different aspects of spiritual leadership.*

OUR INVITATION

WE INVITE the citizens of the world to actively participate in the Three Year Plan of the Spiritual Regeneration Movement:

- *to rise above the cares and worries of daily life*

- *to gain more energy*

- *to accomplish more*

- *to enjoy more*

- *and to enrich all the glories of life—material and spiritual*

WE INVITE individuals as well as *leaders of organizations* to participate in the training program of the Spiritual Regeneration Movement and to learn the theory and practice of Maharishi's simple system of Transcendental Meditation so that they may carry its great benefit to their fellow human beings and the members of their organizations.

WE INVITE the attention of the *education authorities* of different countries—trustees and managing bodies of the universities and colleges—to help their professors receive the training of Meditation Guides so that they may bring the benefits of meditation into the life of their students and help them to easily unfold their latent faculties to become more responsible and more powerful citizens of their countries. Needless to say, that if the children are trained to meditate even 5 to 10 minutes a day they will never develop wrong tendencies, and the growing problem of juvenile delinquency will be eliminated.

WE INVITE the health authorities of all countries—managing bodies of the medical colleges and allied institutions—to create facilities for the study and practice of Transcendental Meditation for all those who are being trained as doctors, nurses, psychiatrists, and all concerned with the mental and physical health of all the people, so that they may bring the healing influence of deep meditation to remove the distress and pain of body and mind.

WE INVITE the *well wishers of public life* everywhere in every part of the world, and the heads of the states and governments of all countries who are anxious to see their people better in every way, to rise to the call of the Spiritual Regeneration Movement, to help erect meditation centers in every corner of human habitation, and to infuse the system of Transcendental Meditation in the daily routine of everyone.

PEACE AND HAPPINESS of the world can be permanent only if the individual is trained to rise above confusion and the worries of life, to the higher values of living. The THREE YEAR PLAN of the Spiritual Regeneration Movement aims at world peace by enlightening the largest number of individuals in the shortest possible time.

TO CARRY OUT the Three Year Plan of the Spiritual Regeneration Movement, cooperation and help are needed from one and all.

Appendix E Transcript of Lecture Given at University of Southern California by Maharishi Mahesh Yogi, May 25, 1959

———•••———

I am happy this morning to be in the company of the students of Southern California. Student life is the time for preparation, preparation for a successful life. This is the time when you have to prepare to have a good body, good mind, good soul, development of all parts in order to live and enjoy life better and insure all betterment hereafter also. Just the preparation of life is the student's career.

As you know the whole field of activity is just a play of the mind. A man who has a strong mind is a more successful man in the world. He achieves more, acquires more, enjoys more. All depends upon the strength of mind. You are studying religion. I am told you are the students of world religion; and by means of comparative study of all religions you aim at having a clear mind about the path that leads to all glory in life.

Religion is the path leading to all development in life, leading to all glories in life, ultimately leading to the eternal glory which is the essential nature of life, eternal bliss. Religion is the direct path to eternal bliss, to salvation.

Philosophy is descriptive. Philosophy describes the nature of the goal of life. Religion provides a path, do this and don't do this, in order that you may have a free entry into the Kingdom of Heaven within. Within and without the realm of heaven the field of eternal bliss is to be experienced. So when it is experienced within, it is also experienced without. Anything that is near and far is easier to achieve at the nearest end. That is why the purpose of all religions is to insure peace, prosperity, and happiness here in the present and insure peace, prosperity, and happiness in the future. That is why the goal of life, the moral goal of life, is a virtuous way of living. Religion tells us how to do this and how to do that, describes virtue, describes sin, encourages to accept virtue, discourages to go towards sin. This is the practical path to salvation; this is the practical path to all development in life. All that is to be done, and its manner of performance is the field of religion. That which is to be achieved as the goal of life, as the result of religious life, is philosophy.

While being introduced I was introduced as one coming from the Shankaracharya Order. The philosophy of Shankara is that all this world is bliss, and I myself am bliss, and nothing else is.

All this is Brahman. Brahman is absolute bliss, eternal bliss, the ultimate reality, the truth of existence. So all this is bliss, and That I am, and That alone is. Except That, there is nothing. There is nothing which is except That, and That is bliss, so all is bliss. This is the philosophy of Shankara.

How to live that in life? Now this is the greatest philosophy of the world. All is bliss; omnipresent is the Kingdom of Heaven. Because you have studied religion and you have seen a little bit of philosophical gymnastics, we will see how all this is bliss, because we are probably thinking the bliss alone is out of sight and everything else is experienced. Misery is experienced, pain is experienced, happiness is also experienced; but that which is called bliss—bliss means happiness of greatest order in permanent nature, happiness that is of greatest intensity and of permanent nature.

When we find everything fleeting and everything changing and nothing seems to be permanent...how can the happiness be permanent and how can everything be happiness? How can this flower be happiness, and how can these leaves be happiness? What does it mean?

Science helps us come to the conclusion that all this is bliss. Shankarian philosophy is not the vain fiction of a crackpot mind. It is the experience of the most scientific minds. We know present day material science, investigation into the field of chemistry, of matter, has declared that all this is nothing but molecules and atoms; and that the atoms are divided into electrons and protons. Electrons and protons are nothing but charges of electricity; so all this is electricity; all this form is nothing but formless electricity. That we cannot dispute. That is established truth of science. So, according to present day science, the ultimate reality of this leaf and the ultimate reality of this flower are nothing but formless electricity, formless energy. So all these forms, all the beauty of the rose, is nothing but a superimposition on that formless energy. All the greenness of the leaf is nothing but a superimposition on the formless energy. So the investigations of science have led us to believe that through all these different forms and designs and colors what we are really experiencing is nothing but formless energy. That is the ultimate reality of matter—formless energy.

Now the form has been abolished and what exists is the energy. So today, on the basis of the findings of material science, we are in a position to say that all this world is nothing but formless energy, although we are seeing all this...and all this.

Ice is nothing but water. Every particle of ice is a particle of water; and ice is water through and through although it is being seen as ice. But it is nothing but water. All these forms and all these different experiences of phenomena are nothing but formless energy. Once we are able to establish the validity of energy as existence, all that exists is energy and nothing else. This is an established fact.

We could further go on in the field of analysis. Now, because matter has been reduced to energy, all these forms have been reduced to the formless. The field of material science is over because the investigations were material science, meaning investigations in the field of matter. Now the matter has come to the end. But that is not all the existence. We know we have the body which is material. Now the reality of the body has been established as energy.

But we have another aspect of our existence, and that is the subjective aspect of our existence. This body is the objective aspect of our existence; mind, intellect, ego, soul, they are the subjective aspect of our existence. So the investigations in the field of material science are only objective. But that is not all the analysis of all that exists in the universe.

If we could have a way to investigate into the subtler phases of analysis, if we could find of what the mind is made and of what the intellect is made and of what the ego is made, then ultimately we will come to the conclusion. So that Brahman, that bliss, is the ultimate reality of which the ego is made, the intellect is made, the mind is made, and then, further on in the field of grosser manifestation, the body is made, and all this limitless vast universe is made. The same one thing, the same one electronic, protonic energy is transformed into the form of the leaf, into the form of the stem, into the form of the flower, into the form of all the different elements, and all the permutations and combinations of the whole universe. So the one, formless energy exhibits itself into different forms. Analysis of the universe taken further ahead: the one blissful, ultimate reality is pervading through all the ego, through all the intellect, through all the mind, through all the body, through all the universe. Here we come to establish the fact that it is one reality, never changing; and that which is the ultimate reality is non-changing.

All the changes take place in the field of relativity—relative order. That which is the ultimate reality of all the relativity is absolute. It never changes; it knows no change; it is ever the same; and its essential nature is bliss consciousness. Bliss consciousness, absolute bliss consciousness, "sat-chit-ananda," Brahman. That is the ultimate reality, and "That alone is," and "That I am," and "That thou art." This is reality of life. This is the reality of all the subjective aspects of life. This is the reality of all the objective aspects of life. Subjective and objective are the two aspects of our personality.

Subjective personality: all the experiences, the experiencer in us—experiencer is composed of impressions through the senses, the mind, the intellect, the ego. And the soul is beyond the subjective and objective aspects. You know, even as you find the objective aspect is changing, subjectivity of our personality is changing. The body is never stable, changing; so also the subjective aspect of our personality is changing. The mind is always seeking, changing. The intellect is always changing; the ego is always changing. So the subjective aspect of personality is also changing, objective aspects of personality are also changing. Both the subjective and objective aspect of man is ever changing.

At the root of all this changing is the never changing principle of life; and That I am; and That is the reality of life. That is never changing, and That we call Brahman in the language of Shankara philosophy. The nature of Brahman is that which Christ said, "The Kingdom of Heaven," "I and the Father are one." That is that level of oneness which knows no duality, transcending all fields of nature, subjective and objective both.

It is the field of the absolute, it is the state of Being, pure state of Being. It is transcendent, transcending all the objective and all the subjective personality—transcendental reality. The nature of it is bliss. Bliss means happiness of greatest order. Now that bliss, because it is the ultimate reality, is omnipresent. It is the ultimate reality of all the gas in the air, the ultimate reality of everything. And that which is the ultimate reality of everything is the essential constituent of everything. If, for example, water is the ultimate reality of ice, then the water is the constituent of ice, and we find that ice is nothing but water.

Because Brahman is the ultimate reality of everything, That, alone, is pervading. That alone is presenting Itself into different degrees as if that abstract, formless thing has manifested

258

Itself into different degrees to become all the names and forms, to become all the phases of the subjective personality of man. Somewhere it has become ego, somewhere it has become intellect, somewhere mind, and somewhere the senses, somewhere the prana, the breath, somewhere the body, somewhere the nails, somewhere the fingers, somewhere the ceiling, somewhere the earth, stones, trees. That has manifested Itself into different degrees. The whole cosmos is nothing but permutations and combinations of the one, unchanging principle as it goes on changing...changing. Now That, in its nature, is bliss. If bliss is universal, if bliss is omnipresent, if bliss is in and out, if bliss is everything, then why has that bliss gone out of experience? This is the question. How can that go out of experience which is in and out—how can that possibly go out of experience?

To answer this "How?" we analyze the machinery of our experience. Machinery of our experience is the mind, and experience is through the senses. Now we know that the senses experience only as long as the objects are gross. When the flower is big, eyes are able to see; if the flower becomes very minute, eyes fail to see, and we need the microscope. When the sound is big, ears are able to hear; when the sound becomes subtle, the ears fail to hear. When the smell is big, gross, the nose is able to smell; when the smell becomes faint, nose fails to smell.

You see, the machinery of our experience is capable of experiencing only the gross aspect of objectivity. Subtle aspects of objectivity the senses do not experience. And because the mind is always engaged in experiencing things through the senses, the mind is capable of enjoying only the gross aspect of nature. Subtle aspect of nature is behind the scene because the machinery is gross.

The senses have not the capacity of experiencing the finer. Eyes cannot see minute things. We need a microscope and bigger microscopes to see the finer things made bigger so that the finest object goes beyond the limit of any of the biggest microscopes. Because mind has been engaged in experiencing things through the senses for a very long time, it is as if the capacity of the mind for experiencing becomes blunt. The subtle field of nature we are not experiencing. All our life is in the field of experiencing the gross glory of nature.

As we know, the power, the beauty, lies in the subtlety of nature. If you hit somebody with this flower, it would hurt, but if you could excite the atom of it, it would explode. The power lies in the subtlety of nature. You break the petal, it produces some energy, some heat energy, but not too much. But if you could split an atom, the whole thing explodes. The power lies in the subtlety of nature, the glory lies in the subtlety of nature, the beauty lies in the subtlety of nature. The subtleties of nature are much more fascinating, more charming, more glorified than the gross field of nature. And as long as we are experiencing only the gross field through the senses, we are limiting our joys of life. The whole field is the material field, gross field and subtle field. The material field and our life through the senses is only in the field of the gross.

Transcendental Meditation is the technique whereby the mind is led on to experience the subtler glories of nature; and then, at every step, the mind experiences greater glory until it experiences the glory of the Transcendent, which is bliss eternal. Because we are experiencing only this side our phase of experience is outward. Outwards and inwards are the expressions only to mean the gross glory of nature and subtle glory of nature. When the mind is somewhere in the middle of nature, the gross glory of nature and the subtle glory of nature, the mind stands to this side. When it is facing this side it has a back towards the greater glories of life; it has a back towards the subtler field of nature. If there could be a way to turn the face of experience there, the mind would go on because greater charm in this life, in this field, naturally attracts the mind.

At every step the mind goes on towards greater glory, enjoying greater and greater glory. Ultimately it enjoys the greatest glory of the form of the sound, the greatest glory of nature at the point-nature, at the point-sound, at the point-form, at the point-smell, and then, the last, transcending that, comes to the field of absolute away from the field of this earth. Inward march is the march towards greater glories of life, toward the greatest glory, permanent glory of life, bliss eternal and absolute.

Just a simple affair outwardly you are experiencing; inside you begin to experience directly your own nature. Experience of our own nature is the experience of the bliss which is absolute and that means the experience of the omnipresent, transcendental reality.

That amounts only to allowing the mind to experience the inner glories of the medium whatever be the medium. You take a form and reduce it until it is reduced to nil thus throwing the mind to the Transcendent.

You take a sound and reduce the sound. You are going to the subtle field of sound, subtler field of sound, coming to this mental disposition. You know, mental disposition is the subtlest sound, but if you could have the technique of reducing the mental disposition

of sound and experience the subtler stages of it in the thought—
mental disposition of sound is just a thought—and if the thought
could be reduced gradually till the thought is reduced to nil
throwing the mind to the Transcendent, this is the way of enjoying greater glories of nature. No mysticism involved in this. The
whole process is the process of direct experience. The whole march
is a scientific march. All that is experienceable, all that can be put
to test for direct experience, is scientific. The whole process of
Transcendental Meditation is just scientific, and it amounts to
experiencing the subtler glories of nature and ultimately enjoying
the glory of the omnipresent.

Because the mind is always engaged in experiencing through the
senses, it is experiencing only the gross field of nature, as if the
capacity of the mind has become blunt. Let it experience some
subtler fields of nature and the capacity of the mind to experience
will be increased, increased, increased. This is the way of
purification of mind. This is the way of sharpening the mind. This
is the way of unfolding all the latent faculties hidden in the ocean
of mind. The whole field of subtle nature is the field of mind. And
the whole field of mind is the ocean of mind, conscious mind,
subconscious mind, super-conscious mind, ultimately the pure
consciousness. And as you allow the mind to experience subtler
phases of your medium you fathom the deeper levels of consciousness and ultimately come to pure consciousness.

This whole field is the field of psychology. But, unfortunately,
the present field of psychology is just skimming the surface of the
ocean of mind. It is the process of Transcendental Meditation
that leads the mind to experience greater charm at every step and

then leads the mind to fathom all the deeper levels of our subconscious mind, ultimately transcending the limit of individual
mind, coming on to the field of cosmic mind, universal mind.
Universal mind is Cosmic Consciousness, and that is omnipresent.
Its nature is bliss.

Devoid of the practice of Transcendental Meditation life becomes a struggle. You know, if you want a man to become a good
swimmer on the surface of the water, it is necessary for him to be
taught to dive. When he goes deep into the water then he swims
well on the surface. If you experience greater glories of life within
and great happiness, you swim on the surface of life much better.
Inner levels of the ocean of mind have to be contacted, subconscious levels of the mind have to be fathomed, then all the faculties
that are latent, all the power, all the latent capacities will come to
the surface.

I wish to teach the people a direct method of taking a dive
within, unfolding all the latent faculties and experiencing that great
bliss in life. Being bliss, when the mind comes out, it comes out full
with energy, full with peace, full with happiness; and then with that
great energy, peace, and happiness, it enjoys the world much better.

The purpose of taking a dive within is to go to the depths of the
sea and gather the pearls there and bring the pearls out to enjoy
their value on the surface. We go within and take a dive and reach
the realms of bliss and let the mind be submerged in It, let the
mind be It, let the mind soak in the bliss as a sponge soaks in, and
then come out full with that great bliss and with greatest satisfaction enjoy the world.

So one way is the march to the Divine, one way is the march

to bliss; the other way is the march of bliss to the world. We go to the Divine and bring the Divine into the world and then the world becomes Divine. And then with this all the faculties of the mind develop, and with the developed faculties of the mind you enjoy the world better. Everywhere will be success. Otherwise life is just limited; and when it is limited nothing satisfies. Then the life becomes a struggle, and we begin to define life as a struggle. Whereas the truth is that life is bliss.

Devoid of the technique of living (the technique of living is just to take a dive into bliss, make the mind blissful, be blissful, and come out with bliss, and then the life is bliss); otherwise, if you are not able to contact the inner chamber of happiness, then all things are disturbing, because nothing in the outside world will be able to satisfy a man. Nothing is so fascinating, so charming, as to satisfy the mind's thirst for happiness. Mind is thirsting for great happiness, wandering here and there and there, just thirsty. And you are told that the mind is a monkey and the mind is so bad and it is not concentrated at all. I completely reject this idea that mind is a monkey. Mind is a king of kings; everybody's mind is a king of kings. To call it a monkey is a bad thing.

Any respectable man needs a proper place to sit. If a king is found walking here and there, it is wrong to conclude that it is the nature of the king to wander. Wandering is not the nature of the king. Poor fellow does not have a proper place to sit. How can he sit? His mind needs a laudable place, a charming place, a place of beauty, a place of great joy, and then it will be resting. Nothing of the world is able to give that great joy which will satisfy. Nothing of the outside glory is the proper peace to the mind, and that is why it

264

goes from this to this, from this to this. And then you feel that you need variety, and variety gives peace. It is a wrong idea. It is not the variety that gives peace. It is inefficiency of glory. The glory is less, and that is why the mind becomes a football of everything kicked from place to place, from place to place.

A thirsty man, not finding water anywhere, begins to taste dew drops deposited on the green grass. Why? Only because no one drop is able to satisfy. He is attracted to the other drop, not because the glory of the drop is attracting him, but because the misery of the first drop deserts him. If the first drop is able to satisfy the mind, then it will not go to the second drop. So it is not due to the glory of the second drop that he is attracted toward it. Misery of the first drop repels him, and he is compelled to go to the second drop. Again it repels, again it repels, so the mind wanders to this, to this, to this, not because the glory is great there, but because the misery was found greater than the first. This is life. Mind is going. Mind is wandering only to settle down somewhere in bliss.

It is wrong to conclude that it is the nature of the mind to wander. It is not wandering; only the outer compulsion is wandering. What else could it do except wander? The nature of the mind is not wandering. It is wandering out of compulsion, not finding any place, any proper seat to sit. And it is wandering to settle down somewhere in bliss.

The very principle is wrong; and then they begin to say that the mind is wandering and then to control the mind. So what is controlling the mind? Mind cannot be controlled on anything that is not charming. Mind cannot be controlled on anything that is not one hundred per cent bliss. A thirsty man, how can he be controlled unless he is given water to satisfy him? Enough water will satisfy and then he is controlled. You run to catch a dog and he runs; and he runs faster and faster, and you reach near him and he bites. It is difficult to control the dog. The best means is to leave a little food at the door and the dog does not go away. Try to satisfy the dog. Satisfying it, you get all advantages of controlling it without any stronger need to control. Here is the technique of controlling the dog. To run after it is only a bad way of controlling the dog.

To try to control the mind without providing any means of greater happiness is a bad technique of control. It is a bad manner to control. It is no way to control and it cannot be controlled. No, the best means is just providing it with something that will satisfy. Again, feed the dog at the door, and for some time he will not leave even if you beat him.

If mind is to be controlled, just lead it to bliss, and it is controlled already. That is why I offer a technique to satisfy the mind and not control the mind. We lead the mind inward; and to lead the mind inward is very natural. The mind is already tired of all things outside. It is already too tired to remain anywhere in the outside world. Just a little turn inward and the inner glories fascinate the mind, and because the field is glorious the mind goes that way. It not only goes, it rushes on to deeper sources. We are listening to some melody, and a better melody comes from a different source. Immediately the mind goes on to that. It is not necessary to train the mind to enjoy greater melody. It takes no long time, no strenuous practice, no training is necessary for the mind to enjoy more, because it is already trying to enjoy more. Just a turn inward, turn, and the mind goes happily. When you proceed toward a light, at every step the light increases. When you lead the mind towards eternal bliss, at every step happiness increases; and that increased happiness is a natural charm to the mind, it enchants the mind, and mind goes that way. Therefore, anybody who says the practice of meditation is difficult, and inward going is very difficult, and Kingdom of Heaven is difficult, and so on and so on, it is all foolish, all on the platform of ignorance, not knowing the nature of the mind.

The nature of the mind is not wandering; the nature of the mind is settled. Had wandering been the nature of the mind then the mind would feel happiness, happy and pleased, if it were allowed to wander more and more. Anything that is done in accord with nature pleases a man. If wandering had been the nature of the mind then he would feel happy and more happy when mind is allowed to wander more and more. But we find when the mind is allowed to wander more, when it does not get anything pleasant to sit on, to enjoy, then it feels miserable, unhappy, discontented. When the mind does not get any proper seat, when the mind does not get any medium of joy, then it wanders from place to place; and wandering makes it miserable; and this leads to the conclusion that wandering is not the nature of the mind. Settling down is the nature of the mind; remaining settled is the nature of the mind. Calm, peace, is the nature of the mind. Mind will be calm and peaceful only if it is settled in bliss. Nothing less than one hundred per cent bliss will satisfy the mind. It will always be searching, searching, searching.

All the present systems of meditation which are prevalent today, all the systems of controlling the mind, they try to refine the mind. As to the methods of refining the mind, I classify them into two systems. I give one analogy. There is a house, a very poor house in very bad condition, downtrodden, all dirty and dull. There are two ways to enter the house. One way is to renovate the house, polish and make it attractive and beautiful so that when you reach it you feel you want to enter it. This I call objective glorification. You glorify the object so that you feel for it; and there you have it, objective glorification.

The other method is subjective refinement. You refine your mind and what do you do? Go to the house and feel the dirt and come back and go again and be repelled and go again to experience the filth of it and come back. Let the mind be used to it, used to it, used to it...dirty, obnoxious...and come back again, so that the dirt becomes the nature of the mind, and some day you ignore it and enter the house. This is subjective refinement. That is, you make your mind used to the medium, whatever it is. This is unpleasant in the beginning, and then when the dirt becomes the nature of the mind it enters the mind.

All the present day practices prevalent in the air for training the mind are just like that. You attract, you attach the mind; somewhere you put the mind. You put the mind here, you put the mind there, you put the mind somewhere, and then the mind rebels; and again you push the mind, and again it comes back. It comes back because it does not find any positive charm there. Not finding any positive charm it is repelled, and it is natural for it to be repelled. Again you push it, and it comes back, and again you push it, and it comes back, so it is just pushing and pushing. All this process becomes a tedious task. When it becomes tedious it takes away life and gives nothing. And when it is tedious people say it is difficult to control the mind, and the path to enlightenment is difficult, and you can't have it unless you are persistently trained for it. They only presume that the glory of the outside world is greater, and the glory of the inner world is much less, so the mind does not want to go to the lesser glory but wants to remain in the greater glory. The whole principle is wrong.

Outside world is not so enchanting and has no capacity of fascinating the mind because the mind is already tired. Nothing of the outside world is able to satisfy. This is the everyday experience. Inside lies the great glory, but the method of approach to that glory is wrong. You are facing this side and enjoying the drops. This side is a great pond. Unless you turn about, it is not possible to be fascinated by the other side. What you do is turn thirty degrees, the same misery, and then sixty degrees and the same misery. The glory lies in turning completely, one hundred eighty degrees. Immediately turn and you are there, and you will begin to turn gradually ten degrees, thirty degrees, ninety degrees, one hundred thirty degrees. All this turning amounts to greater misery. If not greater, then misery is equal. This side is drops of misery, this side also. You don't find anything more than a drop. The mind was going from drop to drop because the pond is just one hundred eighty degrees. The finer the outside world, the finer the inner nature. So just adjust this other side. It should be instantaneous.

I hear in this country Zen is much talked about, and they speak of instantaneous enlightenment. But, unfortunately, there is no Zen master today who could give instantaneous enlightenment. The theory is all right; that bliss is omnipresent, it is already there; and I am That, and Thou art That, and why not have it straight away. But there should be a way. Mind needs to be refined, and the mind will be refined because the mind is experiencing the gross in order to be able to experience the subtle. In order to be able to experience the Transcendent the mind should be able to experience all the subtler stages, and then it experiences That. So just turn about and begin to experience the subtler stages of the medium, a positive medium, and begin to experience the subtler phases of the medium. Experiencing the subtler stages you come on to experience the Transcendent straight away.

So almost all the practices of meditation belonging to all groups and all religions today, they try to turn by degrees and the mind is not satisfied. When the mind is not satisfied then the intelligent man thinks it is a waste of time and why bother.

You go to the tennis court, and one hour you devote there, and you feel positively you are enjoying something. You sit, closing the eyes, talking over nothing, and you feel what is it? Why waste time? That is why the tendency of the age is shifting. People shift from going inward because the direction is not proper. The direction, the guidance, is not proper. To give this direct guidance and proper training to the people, I have started the Spiritual Regeneration Movement, and that is to spiritually regenerate the whole world through this simple process of Transcendental Meditation which directly gives a turn of one hundred eighty degrees to the mind, and the mind enjoys this. This amounts to all experiences of the inward life. All faculties of mind, the whole field of psychology is gained, the whole field of philosophy is achieved. This is the philosophy of Shankara. To enable everybody to experience this, I have come out with this simple technique. This is the practical glory of Indian philosophy. All the past claims of Indian philosophy are this: that all this is bliss, and That I am. Here is a technique to experience it, to be blissful. This fulfills the purpose of religion. This fulfills the commandments of all the great masters of religion.

Christ said, "First ye seek the Kingdom of God and all else will be added unto thee." This is the Kingdom of God, the Kingdom of Heaven. Just seek the Kingdom of Heaven and then all else will be added on because the mind becomes so powerful. Bliss, contented thought force, becomes so great. How does the thought force become great? When the mind experiences great happiness it is contented. When it is contented it does not bother about much. When it does not bother energy is saved. Otherwise, if the mind is discontented, not contented, energy is dissipated. Thinking ten thousand thoughts a minute, afterward ten thoughts,—then each thought has a capacity of a thousand thoughts—plus the strength. This is how will power increases, thought force increases, greater happiness comes; and this is the fulfillment of life. This is the state of Nirvana in the language of Buddha. That is the state of the Kingdom of Heaven according to Christ. That is Jivan Mukti, Cosmic Consciousness, that great silence of the Transcendent to be lived in life even when you are busily engaged in the activity of the diversity. That is Nirvana, that is Jivan Mukti, that is the Kingdom of Heaven; that is the goal of all religions and that fulfills the purpose of all education.

Education is unfoldment of the inner capabilities, inner faculties of man. And unless the mind is drawn within, unless the attention is drawn within to fathom all the deeper levels of subconscious mind, the education will always be incomplete. This is the fulfillment of all branches of learning, all branches of science, of scientific investigation into the truth; and this is the truth scientific of all that exists in the world. This is the fulfillment of all philosophy, this is the goal of all religions. In one stroke of Transcendental Meditation the fulfillment of life is achieved.

Now I think my time is up and I have given you, in short, the synopsis of the whole of life and the purpose of it and the way to achieve it.

Now I would like to answer your questions.

QUESTIONS & ANSWERS

Q. Are there certain things that you must give up?

A. What is there to be given up in order to enjoy the great glory lying behind? What is to be given up? Only let us go in and come out. Nothing is to be given up. You know, when a man is living in a small hut, and he is transferred to a palace, we do not count it to be a loss of the hut because a palace is gained. It is no loss. If a man conducting a business earns ten thousand dollars a year and he goes on to earn a million dollars a year, what has he lost? It is not a loss of ten thousand dollars, it is an addition of a million dollars—so we do not count it a loss. What it means is, just sit for some time and enjoy and then come up. The theory of renunciation and theory of detachment are not for the people of the world. If the bliss is omnipresent, if the Kingdom of Heaven is just within me, then that which is within me should be lived naturally even when the eyes are enjoying this and this and this. That which is within me should be lived naturally even when the eyes are busily engaged in enjoying the outer glories of nature. Those who advocate "leave this and then you will get that," and "leave the joys of the world in order to get the joy of the soul," and all that, they only say, unless you put out this light how can you have the bright sunlight in the room? It is a bad logic. Put out this light…as long as you have this light, how can you have the brighter sunlight? I say remaining in this light, by the aid of this light open the door, and the bright sunlight will be in. To allow the bright sunlight in is solely to open the door, and it is not necessary to put out the light.

Those who say that you renounce this and you renounce that,

they think that the glory of this is great, and unless the greater glory is given out how will the mind go to the field of lesser glory? So they presuppose that the world is more glorified and presuppose that the glory of God is much less than the glory of the world. So greater glory you lose and then only the mind will accept—in the absence of the great glory of the world the mind is miserable and will accept the lesser glory of God. The theory of detachment is based on this only, that the world is glorified and is fascinating and is enchanting the mind, and unless you shut the doors of the world how can you enjoy the Divine? But it is bad logic. The field of the Divine is like the bright sunlight outside. The field of the world is like the small electric light inside the room. Although it seems to be sufficient, the self sufficiency of this light is only as long as the doors are not open. Remaining in the field of the world, enjoying all the glories of material life, just let the inner door be open, just for the sake of experience, just for a few minutes enter That, and that is that.

The things of the world need a long time to achieve because they are the things of the outside. You have to achieve. You go to the office, you go and come, you go and come and then earn something. So anything that is far away from you needs greater strength and greater time. That which is within only needs going there and enjoying just a few minutes. Then having gone there there are two other things: one, nothing is required to be lost in the world and no sense of detachment is necessary—that is one thing. The other, which is of a greater value, is the brightness of the world will be increased by the light of the inner self. Not that the material and spiritual values go hand in hand, but, with the experience of the inner light, outer glories will further be brightened.

That is the value of spiritual development. You directly experience it and then enjoy the world better. Here is a means to enjoy the world better and not forgo the joys of the world.

Q. What is the "awareness of self consciousness"?

A. Awareness of self consciousness, self awareness, is a state of Being, and this state of Being is that state where nothing else could distract it.

For example, a student has been declared passed in the class and the joy of passing has filled his nature, and by nature he is happy. He is happy talking to others and going around here and there even when he is not aware of passing. Even though intellectually he does not hold the idea of passing yet he enjoys the result of passing. So even if there is no intellectual idea of self awareness, that state of Being is. And one lives that through all the experiences of life.

Cosmic Consciousness is the state which lives that eternal silence in the midst of all activity. No activity is able to make it less; no silencing of the activity will make it more. The state of Being is absolute in its nature and not related to any of the outside experiences. Therefore, nothing of the outside world is able to make it less or more. And this is the result of a few minutes. Take a dive to the deeper levels of consciousness and come out, go and come out, go and come out. With the practice of going in and coming out, of contacting the Divine more and more, more and more of the peace and happiness and energy comes out, and ultimately one hundred per cent of it comes out; and then in and out becomes the same. In and out has no difference. Remaining full-fledged in the field of activity that eternal peace is lived in life. So that state of self awareness is not the state completely devoid of energy and activity and experience. Through all experience it is lived.

Q. I think of something you told me when we talked before. One of the things we are interested in is that you feel this enables a person to deal with relative problems much better, say problems that are economic. It doesn't solve them, but you can meet them much better?

A. Yes. A contentious mind doesn't get to peace. And you will find the means of earning is much better with a contented mind. A more spiritual mind has greater energy. If the individual's mind is discontented and distressed, devoid of energy, then he would eat anything; and eating anything he might fall sick. So that eating may not be worth anything at all. With more energy, with a clear, satisfied mind, he would not eat just anything, he would eat something good.

Q. What exactly is the state of mind during Transcendental Meditation?

A. It is difficult to express that but one analogy I will give you. A good friend of yours for ten years lives in New York and you want very much to see him. When suddenly he comes to see you, how much you begin to feel joy, and joy fills the whole heart. This feeling of elation taken to a million times is that. Because this is a thing of relative order, and that is a thing of the absolute, it makes the mind just full with That, so the effect of it lasts the whole day, for many days, for a whole lifetime. Just like that.

Q. What I meant was, what exactly is the mind doing?

A. The mind is experiencing. Experiencing means, for example, flower...flower...flower...flower...flower...flower. What is the mind doing here? It is experiencing different volumes of sound...flower ...experiencing different volumes of sound. There the mind is experiencing different stages of thought, subtler stages of thought.

Here in Transcendental Meditation we do not say, "I'm going to bliss," "I'm going to bliss," "I'm going to bliss"; all this is superficial, hypnosis, self-hypnosis. "I'm going to bliss," "I'm going to bliss," and then begin to feel bliss. That is an imposed thought of bliss. This is self-hypnosis. Self-hypnosis is that which excites emotional feeling and completely blocks off the intellectual aspects. So although we could say, "I am a king," "I am a king," "I am a king," the truth is that intellect knows that I am not a king; but intellect is blocked, not allowed to function. And the emotions are excited so much that you begin to feel kingship. This is the idea, a manipulated idea of kingship, not the real state of the king!

Hypnotism blocks off intellectual aspects of mind and excites the emotions. You are not in that state but you feel you are in that state. Practices of hypnotism are a great loss to efficiency of man because they block off the intellectual aspect. They begin to feel something. You are not actually sleeping, but you feel "I am sleepy." You are not sleeping, but you feel "I am sleeping." That is why in the morning you do not get up as fresh as you could get up. The peace that you feel after getting up is just superficial peace which is dispelled after one or two hours.

This practice of Transcendental Meditation develops all faculties of intellect simultaneously along with all faculties of emotion. Emotions are made perfect, intellect is made perfect—the whole personality is integrated.

Q. Do you use flowers in your system of Transcendental Meditation?

A. No. Flowers are seen. A goldsmith sees the design, the cut, and then he evaluates the value of gold simultaneously. Seeing the design his vision is trained to evaluate the value of gold...this is sixteen karat, fourteen karat. Not that when he evaluates the gold at sixteen or fourteen karats he doesn't see the form. It is the form that enables him to evaluate the value. It is the design, the form, that helps him to evaluate.

So the glory is that the unmanifest absolute abstract is enjoyed through the sight of the manifested relative objectivity. This is the utility of objectivity, this is the value of duality. The field of duality enables the joy of unity through life. Otherwise you are often told that this is the duality—that is a misery.

I say, having contacted unity of life, it is the field of duality that enables one to find that unity through all experiences of life. This is the glory. And this is the great Shankara philosophy. Generally, I do not speak in public in terms of Shankara philosophy because it has been more misrepresented in terms of renunciation and detachment. This is Vedanta which speaks of universality of bliss through all the diversities of nature, through all the different experiences. This is real Vedanta; and this is the purpose of Yoga. The purpose of Yoga is to turn the mind one hundred eighty degrees inward and then let the mind be in bliss. And the purpose of Vedanta is to tell you intellectually that you were experiencing that bliss in the transcendental state; and when you come out, you are coming out somewhat in that bliss, somewhat in that silence, until you are living that silence. This information is given by Vedanta. So this is Yoga. One-way march of meditation is Vedanta which enables self-consciousness to become Cosmic Consciousness. The inner march of the mind is to self-consciousness, the purpose of Yoga, and the outer march of the mind from the Divine to the world is the way of Vedanta–Cosmic Consciousness from the platform of self-consciousness. From self-consciousness to Cosmic Consciousness is the field of Vedanta. From the objective consciousness to the self-consciousness is the field of Yoga. Both of them are handled in one stroke of Transcendental Meditation.

This is the message of the Spiritual Regeneration Movement, and for this purpose I am establishing Transcendental Meditation Centers everywhere. This is the way to integrate life, to enjoy life in all its various aspects, to enjoy life in its fullest glory, all in one stroke of Transcendental Meditation.

JAI GURU DEV

Appendix F Endorsements from Practitioners of World Religions

---

Christian Lutheran Tradition

You are fortunate to be holding this book. I remember when I picked up its second edition in 1979. I expected to wade through a dry history that would enrich my doctoral research in the fields of prayer and meditation. Instead, I was carried away by words of sweetness and light. The language was so simple and innocent, moving me with the power of an ocean wave into a realm of love and grace and peace.

The words of Helena Olson embraced me into the spirit of her family and attracted me to the charm of her home on 433 South Harvard Boulevard in Los Angeles. From the beginning of her book to the end, I felt as if I were experiencing a new life through her. From her first notice of Maharishi to a tear-filled farewell, the reader enters a rare and serene world. Her last page gives a wonderful summary:

...I knew I could not say anything. There was too much to be thankful for: his presence in our home; the laughter in the rooms; the puzzled looks on his face as he tried to understand us; the comedies and anxieties he

shared with us; the chants in the bath; the play with the children and the Siamese cats; the beautiful, flower-filled days; the big, happy family that assembled about him. All this he had brought us, and even more important, the sacred, quiet peace of the soul. (pp. 196-197)

I found my favorite moments in the book (as you may find yours): Helena's first encounter with Maharishi (p. 28); the ripple of laughter when Maharishi says, "Bliss is everywhere. What is needed is only a few minutes morning and evening to go to the treasure, come out and spend in the market place" (p. 43); when Maharishi gives one of his amazing little insights, referring to necessary work you do not like: "See the job. Do the job. Stay out of the misery" (p. 60); when Helena and her family settle in at home with Maharishi (pp. 50-70); when Maharishi explains that "Life is essentially bliss" (p. 153).

Few biographies have touched me with as much joy and emotional sensitivity as Helena's: *The Story of My Life*, by Helen Keller; *Something Beautiful for God: Mother Teresa of Calcutta*, by Malcolm Muggeridge; the Holy Gospels of Jesus Christ. I anticipate that you will come to love Helena's book as much as I do.

The beauty and wisdom of Maharishi's teaching holds a promise of wide range for the Christian community. For those who wish to use the Transcendental Meditation technique as a purely psychological technique, Maharishi preserves the option of a scientific approach so it may be practiced by persons of any religious persuasion. In this regard, the Transcendental Meditation technique may be used to lower blood pressure, reduce anxiety, treat asthma, or lessen dependency on nicotine or alcohol, among other potential benefits.

For scholars who wish to explore the religious implications of the Transcendental Meditation technique, rich mines of meaning may be explored in the context of Maharishi's teaching: detailing the methodologies of prayer, coming to the peace of God, experiencing the nature of grace, entering the kingdom of heaven, or engaging a dialogue between the Vedic and Judeo-Christian understandings of divinity.

I invite you to begin reading the charming story of Maharishi Mahesh Yogi's first visit to the United States of America. While not everyone will appreciate every word in precisely the same way, nor would we wish them to, it is my hope that all people everywhere will find something to learn and to love in these pages of joy and peace.

The Rev. Dr. John R. Reigstad
On the occasion of the visit of Pope John Paul II to St. Louis
January 26-27, 1999

John Reigstad, Ph.D. graduated from St. Olaf College in 1968 and received the Master of Divinity degree from Luther Seminary in 1975. He learned the Transcendental Meditation technique after seeing Maharishi's picture on the Oct. 13, 1975 cover of Time *magazine. Reigstad was ordained in 1977 and awarded the Doctor of Ministry degree from Luther Seminary in 1985. He currently serves American Lutheran Church of Jesup, Iowa; teaches world religions at Wartburg College; and pursues research in consciousness at Maharishi University of Management.*

Roman Catholic Tradition

Since the 1950s, there have been an increasing number of significant contacts between Christians and leaders of Eastern spiritual traditions. Pope John Paul II made an historic visit to the Dalai Lama during the papal visit to India in 1986. Christian monks have held many exchanges with Buddhist and Hindu monks, one of the most famous being those between Thomas Merton and D.T. Suzuki. Such dialogue has revealed remarkable areas of convergence along with the well-known differences among traditions.

Perhaps no Eastern practice has been more widely practiced by Christians than the Transcendental Meditation technique, and no Eastern master more studied than Maharishi Mahesh Yogi. Christian writers have attempted to do with Maharishi's teachings what Thomas Aquinas did with those of Aristotle, namely, to find what is useful for Christian theory and practice.

Maharishi has helped me and many other Christians to rediscover one of the great and often forgotten Christian truths, namely, that contemplative experience provides a powerful foundation for Christian life. Pure contemplation is the experience of the "center of the soul" (in Biblical terminology, "the heart")—an experience of interior silence related by all Christian spiritual masters. They teach that the interior of the soul is not empty, but that the Lord dwells within. St. Teresa of Avila describes contemplation as "a foretaste of the Kingdom of God." For many Christians who are aware of the contemplative tradition the question is, how can I settle my mind? How can I dispose myself for contemplation?

Even though the Transcendental Meditation technique is not a religious technique per se, it has great value for Christian spirituality in that it provides a simple, effortless way for the mind to experience deep silence—a silence that disposes us to contemplation and to knowing the will of God that is written on the human heart (Jeremiah 31:33). Clearly, the TM technique is not sufficient for Christian spirituality. Maharishi himself teaches that his Transcendental Meditation leads one to knowledge of the true self, while prayer, worship, and devotion lead one to God. But a meditation technique that helps develop the mind and heart can only make it more possible to fulfill the fundamental Biblical commandment to "Love the Lord, your God, with all your heart, with all your soul, and with all your mind" (Matthew 22:37).

Father Kevin P. Joyce
St. Maria Goretti Church
San Jose, CA
smgc@pacbell.net

Father Kevin Joyce, Ph.D. has practiced the Transcendental Meditation technique since 1970 and was ordained as a priest in 1980. He completed a Ph.D. in religion at the Catholic University of America in 1991, during which he conducted research on Transcendental Meditation. Father Joyce is now pastor of a large multicultural parish in San Jose, California.

Jewish Tradition

One of the great Hasidic masters taught, "God, where can I find You? And where can I not find You?" For most people, God is an unknown reality: "God, where can I find You?" Lacking a technique for direct experience of the Transcendent—the foundation for living a truly balanced life of the spirit—we tend to flee to the extremes of spiritual seeking: religious fundamentalism, on one hand, and secular materialism on the other. Unfortunately, neither path can provide the freedom and fulfillment that it seems to promise. In its attempt to make one single religion ultimately meaningful, religious fundamentalism inevitably demeans everything else. On the other hand, in its glorification of the transient values and pleasures of material life, secular materialism inevitably demeans the human spirit, and the whole of spiritual life.

"And where can I not find You?" The reality of life, as Maharishi has expounded it over the past 40 years, is that the Infinite can be experienced and enjoyed at every finite point of creation. This can be true for anyone, regardless of his/her beliefs, background, or education. Only one crucial piece is necessary: regular practice of the Transcendental Meditation technique. The TM technique brings one into direct contact with infinite creativity, intelligence, knowledge, and bliss. The result is a life increasingly saturated with the Divine values of universal love, compassion, ethics, and ultimately, devotion to the one, universal God.

There is no shortage of great scripture in the world. There is also an abundance of great religion, theology, and philosophy based on these scriptures. However, there is a profound shortage of individuals capable of living the values of love and compassion espoused by religion, theology, and philosophy. In the *Midrash*—the ancient Rabbinic commentaries on the Bible—God provocatively declares, "Would that mankind would reject Me, but behave according to My Instruction!"

Every religious individual experiences the gap between what God expects of them, and their ability to fulfill those expectations. The TM technique helps to bridge this gap, by bringing individual awareness into direct contact with its Transcendental source—the infinite source of all scripture, religion, theology, and morality. In my experience, I have found nothing simpler or more powerful than the TM technique for making God the living reality of one's life—a reality that can be experienced in every impulse of thought, speech, and action.

The potential for living a fulfilled life in God Consciousness, pervaded by the unity of God, is built into the very nature of a human being. May the day soon come when the leaders and followers of every religion on earth will be able to live together in harmony. Perhaps then, they will be able to point to the same unified, Transcendent reality and say, "This is my God, and I will glorify Him; My father's God, and I will exalt Him" (Exodus 15:2).

Rabbi Alan Green
Beth Israel Synagogue
Winnipeg, Manitoba
Greenrab@pangea.ca

Rabbi Alan Green was instructed in the Transcendental Meditation technique in 1971 and became a teacher of the TM program soon afterward. He was inspired to study for the rabbinate after reading a book on Kabbalah—Jewish mysticism—in which he discovered an extensive Jewish terminology for many of the experiences that Maharishi had introduced during his teacher training course. Rabbi Green was ordained in 1991 and serves as rabbi of Beth Israel Synagogue of Winnipeg, Manitoba.

Hindu Tradition

Learning Maharishi Transcendental Meditation is completely compatible with practicing any religion, including Hinduism. As a Hindu who grew up in a spiritual family, I can say with certainty that Maharishi Transcendental Meditation enhances all aspects of life. When I started practicing TM, our family yagyas started to mean more to me. I also began acting in accord with the laws of Dharma in a very spontaneous and blissful way. My life today is like being cradled in the lap of Mother Nature without any worry whatsoever.

The most remarkable experience I've had was attending Maharishi International University (now known as Maharishi University of Management), in which over forty countries were represented in the student body. While we looked different, spoke many languages and were from various cultures, we all felt that we were basically the same; and that the underlying similarity was consciousness. We also realized that the teachings of our different religions were essentially the same.

I encourage anyone who might be interested in learning Maharishi Transcendental Meditation to do so. Please don't let religion be a barrier to gaining so much more in life. I feel honored and lucky that I have come across TM in this lifetime and have enjoyed practicing it along with my religion for the last twenty years. When you learn to meditate, you will have a more profound experience and understanding of the true nature of all religions.

Mrs. Sooneeta Chuttoorgoon Eisner
B.S. Psychology, Maharishi University of Management
Housewife and member of the Global Development Council for
Maharishi's Transcendental Meditation Movement.

Born in Mauritius, Sooneeta Eisner is a lifelong Hindu who learned the Transcendental Meditation technique in 1979 and became a teacher of this technique in 1989. Eisner holds a Bachelor's degree in Psychology from MIU (now Maharishi University of Management) and has published research on field independence in children. She lives in Fairfield, Iowa, where she is a homemaker, supporter of TM programs and active member of the Indian community.

Islam Tradition

I have been practicing Transcendental Meditation since 1978. Thanks to my practice, I have found, as a Muslim, that with time I gained ever deeper insights into the words of the Holy Koran and of the Hadith, Prophet Mohamed's commentaries. This growing appreciation of the sublime yet practical message of Islam, has afforded me over the years countless experiences of powerful, awe-inspiring, tender devotion towards God Almighty. It is as if His words and those of His Prophet, Peace be upon him, come alive with ever-renewed freshness whenever I read them. This has been a blessing for me in a time of deep questioning and soul searching which we witness in the vast Islamic world community.

There are as many Islams as there are Muslims. This is befitting since Islam is essentially a faith where man and God have a direct relationship between them, without intermediaries, and where God challenges man to personally strive to know Truth. This is why, the Prophet, P.B.U.H., said, "The search for knowledge is incumbent upon every Muslim man and woman." Through personal experience, I have found that the highest knowledge comes from within, from the daily direct experience of Transcendental Consciousness, which is nothing other than the most settled, quietest state of my own consciousness. This loftiest of states brings peace, is peace. I have thus discovered that surrendering to the Almighty is simply a state of mind, of consciousness, which bestows the blessing of supreme peace. This is the truth contained in the two meanings of the word Islam: Surrender and Peace.

Surrender to God to gain Peace. In this wonderful state of total surrender and peace, the heart melts; the mind shines with the light of wisdom, and God begins to reveal Himself.

Wadi Bounouar
Quebec, Canada
wbounouar@ccapcable.com

Originally from Morocco, Wadi Bounouar, a lifelong Muslim, started the Transcendental Meditation technique in 1978. He is now a professional translator in Quebec, Canada.

Buddhist Tradition

I cannot represent Buddhism. I can only speak of Buddhism as a part of my life. The Buddhist message of loving kindness and compassion has always been very powerful for me. By developing my compassion, I not only create a heart connection with other living beings; I also provide a path for my own fulfillment, breaking the grips of the roller coaster of selfish desire.

Buddhism, as I have been taught it, is also deeply pragmatic and open. When, after the Chinese invasion of Tibet in 1950, The Dalai Lama was "invited" to the Chinese capital in Beijing, he traveled with an open mind to learn what Chinese communism had to offer to the understanding of a truly compassionate state. This open mind is fundamental to the Buddhist perspective. The Buddhist tradition has offered me a rich resource for developing my own heart. But it is not in a competition for having the best of everything for every circumstance in all eternity. Rather it directs an unqualified commitment to obtain and manifest the heart of universal compassion through every vehicle available. If otherwise, Buddhism deteriorates into another social identity, separating us from each other as well as our true universal nature.

It is from this background that I warmly embrace the Transcendental Meditation technique as an adjunct to my religious practices. As an individual, the Transcendental Meditation technique has provided me a deep rest that has improved my health, and contributed to an open heart and more effective functioning. As a social scientist investigating Maharishi Transcendental Meditation, I have studied the scientific records that show how a purified nervous system provides the grounds for developing a full heart and practical efficacy.

But what really goes to the core of my heart as a Buddhist is the ability to practice in a group the Transcendental Meditation technique and its more advanced TM-Sidhi program, to dissolve the social tensions of a society and thereby contribute to the well-being of literally millions of people. I have talked to classmates who have traveled with a group of meditators into war-torn countries, sat down as a group and practiced Maharishi Transcendental Meditation, and seen the bombing stop. I have personally examined the research which has systematically documented time and time again the power of this technology to stop wars, reduce crime, cut accident rates, revive economies and otherwise restore the heart and vitality to social systems.

As Buddhists we have the cosmology to understand this phenomenon, the psychological tools to transcend the social inertia dismissing it, and the compassionate heart to act on it. I warmly invite you, and everyone else, to investigate the Transcendental Meditation technique and its technologies for yourself, and join me in creating peace on earth.

Paul Frank
Graduate student at Maharishi University of Management
Fairfield, Iowa
pvfrank@mum.edu

Paul Frank learned Transcendental Meditation in 1975. He has practiced Tibetan Buddhism since 1982. In 1994, after reading the research on the Maharishi Effect which found dramatic positive effects resulting from the group practice of advanced Transcendental Meditation techniques, Frank moved to Fairfield, Iowa, where he is currently a graduate student in psychology at Maharishi University of Management, with a special interest in studying and promoting the Maharishi Effect.

Appendix G Major Achievements of
Maharishi's Movement Throughout the World*

1956 Maharishi tours South India and establishes the first
Spiritual Development Center

1957 Maharishi inaugurates the Spiritual Regeneration
Movement in Madras, India

1958 Maharishi begins his world tours

1959 First International Conference on Transcendental
Meditation; Sequoia National Park, U.S.A.

1961 First Transcendental Meditation Teacher Training
Course, India

1962 Maharishi conducts world-wide courses to train teachers

---

* These highlights are taken from two booklets: Maharishi Vedic
University: Exhibition (1993) and Maharishi Global Development Fund (1997). Please refer to these publications for detailed
information regarding Maharishi's monumental achievements
during the past forty years.

1963 Maharishi writes *Science of Being and Art of Living*

1964 Maharishi writes *Love and God*

1965 Maharishi writes his commentary on the *Bhagavad-Gita*

1966 Maharishi inaugurates his first International Academy of Meditation in India

Inauguration of first European Meditation Academy in Bremen, Germany

1968 Students International Meditation Society inaugurated world-wide

1969 Maharishi begins his translation and commentary on *Brahma Sutras*

1970 First scientific paper on Transcendental Meditation published in *Science* Magazine

1971 Maharishi International University founded in U.S.A.

1972 Inauguration of World Plan in Mallorca, Spain

1973 2000 World Plan Centers established world-wide

1974 Scientists discover that one percent of a city's population practicing the Transcendental Meditation technique improves the quality of city life, a phenomenon now known as the Maharishi Effect

1975 Inauguration of the dawn of the Age of Enlightenment in Switzerland

Maharishi European Research University founded in Switzerland

1976 Maharishi inaugurates his World Government of the Age of Enlightenment

Maharishi introduces his TM-Sidhi program and begins to train Governors of the Age of Enlightenment

1977 Maharishi inaugurates his Ideal Society Campaign in 108 countries

1978 Inauguration of a global undertaking to bring Invincibility to Every Nation

1979 First World Peace Assembly of Governors of the Age of Enlightenment held in U.S.A.

1980 Maharishi brings to light the nature and structure of the Veda through his commentary on Rik Veda, his *Apaurusheya Bhashya*

1981 First International Vedic Science Course held in New Delhi, India with over 3000 Governors of the Age of Enlightenment from around the world participating

1982 Maharishi University of Natural Law inaugurated in England

1983 Maharishi celebrates the Silver Jubilee of his TM Movement

Quantum field theoretical physicists identify and proclaim the Unified Field of all the Laws of Nature to be the same as Maharishi's transcendental field of Consciousness, leading to Maharishi's celebrating the rising sunshine of the Age of Enlightenment throughout the world

Maharishi holds the First World Peace Assembly in U.S.A. (the Global Taste of Utopia Course) with 7000 Governors of the Age of Enlightenment attending, creating a Global Maharishi Effect

1984 Maharishi formulates Unified Field Based Systems of Education, Health, Government, Economics, Defense, Rehabilitation and Agriculture to perpetuate an ideal civilization

1985 Maharishi Vedic University inaugurated in Washington, D.C., U.S.A. in which Maharishi introduces his Vedic Science^{SM} and Technologies for creating an ideal Vedic society

Maharishi reintroduces Maharishi Ayur-Veda to the world and establishes Maharishi Ayur-Veda Prevention Centers throughout the world

Maharishi creates Veda-Lila^{SM}, the "play" of the Veda, which creatively explains the mechanics of creation from its unified unmanifest basis to its innumerable manifest qualities

1986 Maharishi begins a World Plan for Perfect Health to create a disease-free society through his Ayur-Veda

Maharishi creates his Program to Create World Peace which calls for 7000 Vedic Scientists to be trained in India for creating and maintaining world peace

1987 Global Festivals of Music for World Peace held in over 200 cities in 52 countries, presenting Maharishi Gandharva Veda℠ music, Vedic melodies which create balance and harmony in Nature

1988 Maharishi inaugurates a Master Plan to Create Heaven on Earth

1989 Second step of Global Maharishi Effect inaugurated to eradicate poverty throughout the world

1990 Alliance with Nature's Government offered to every Nation

1991 A program is launched to establish Maharishi Ayur-Veda Health Centers in every community

First group of 7000 Yogic Flyers established in the World Capital of the Age of Enlightenment, India

1992 Maharishi Vedic University curriculum offered in ten countries

Maharishi presents his Constitution of the Universe as an addendum to his Vedic treatise on politics

Maharishi celebrates Ram Raj— the rise of perfection in the field of governmental administration

The Natural Law Party, a political party to improve the quality of national administration, is established

1993 Maharishi discovers a formula for creating perfection in every country: he recommends establishing "A Group for a Government"— a large group of Vedic Scientists and Yogic Flyers for every country

1994 Maharishi introduces his Vedic Technology of Defense in which he suggests that the military of each country develop a Prevention Wing composed of Yogic Flyers which will disallow the birth of an enemy

New prevention-oriented programs of Maharishi Ayur-Veda introduced world-wide

1995 Maharishi University of Management established in Japan, Holland, Russia and U.S.A.

Maharishi Corporate Revitalization Program^{SM} introduced to companies in India, Europe, U.S.A. and Australia

Maharishi launches a world-wide program to alert each country to the hazards of modern medicine

1996 Maharishi inaugurates a program to establish Global Administration through Natural Law

1997 Maharishi establishes twelve Time-Zone Capitals for his TM Movement around the world

Maharishi Vedic Medical Council established in India

Maharishi Vedic Medical Associations established in other countries

Vedic Principles of Construction brought to light in Maharishi Sthapatya Veda^{SM}—Vastu Vidya^{SM}

Maharishi Global Development Fund inaugurated

1998 Maharishi Vedic Vibration Technology^{SM} program is inaugurated world-wide

Maharishi Open University (satellite television) Distance Education degree programs begin, targeting every country in the world

Groundbreaking ceremony held for the construction of the world's tallest building in India

1999 First Country of World Peace established in the world near Brazil

Appendix H How to Learn More about
the *Maharishi Transcendental Meditation* Technique
and Advanced Programs

——————————•◆•——————————

TM TRAINING COURSES

The Transcendental Meditation Program in the United States
1-800-LEARN TM http://www.tm.org

TM SCHOOLS AND UNIVERSITIES

Maharishi School of the Age of Enlightenment in the U.S.A.
http://www.mum.edu/maharishi_school

Maharishi University of Management in the U.S.A.
http://www.mum.edu

Maharishi Vedic Universities and Schools in the U.S.A.
http://www.maharishi.org

Maharishi Open University http://www.mou.org

TM AND HEALTH

Maharishi Medical Centers in the US.A.
http://www.maharishi-medical.com

The Maharishi Vedic Approach to Health Chronic Disease Program http://www.vedic-health.com

Maharishi Ayur-Veda® Products sold in the U.S.A.
http://www.mapi.com

The Raj—Luxury Maharishi Medical Center in Fairfield, Iowa, U.S.A. http://www.theraj.com

Maharishi Vedic Vibration Technology
http://www.vedic-health.org

TM AND REHABILITATION

The TM Program and Rehabilitation in the U.S.A.
http://www.mum.edu/rehabilitation.html

TM ADVANCED PROGRAMS

Yogic Flying at Maharishi University of Management, U.S.A.
http://www.yogicflying.org/index.html

®Maharishi Vedic Approach to Health, Maharishi International University, Maharishi University of Management, Maharishi Ayur-Veda, Maharishi Gandharva Veda, Science of Creative Intelligence, Maharishi School of the Age of Enlightenment, Time-Zone Capital, Veda-Lila, Maharishi Vedic University, Maharishi Corporate Revitalization Program, Maharishi Stapathya Veda, Vastu Vidya, Maharishi Vedic Vibration Technology and Maharishi Medical Center are registered or common law trademarks licensed to Maharishi Vedic Education Development Corporation and used with permission.

www.ingramcontent.com/pod-product-compliance
Lightning Source LLC
Chambersburg PA
CBHW031236090426
42742CB00007B/223